CONCILIUM

Religion in the Eighties

CONCILIUM

Editorial Directors

Giuseppe Alberigo	Bologna	Italy
Gregory Baum	Montreal	Canada
Willem Beuken SJ	Nijmegen	The Netherlands
Leonardo Boff	Petrópolis	Brazil
Paul Brand	Ankeveen	The Netherlands
Antoine van den Boogaard	Nijmegen	The Netherlands
Ann Carr	Chicago, Ill.	USA
Marie-Dominique Chenu OP	Paris	France
Julia Ching	Toronto	Canada
John Coleman SJ	Berkeley, Ca.	USA
Mary Collins OSB	Wake Forest, NC	USA
Yves Congar OP	Paris	France
Christian Duquoc OP	Lyons	France
Virgil Elizondo	San Antonio, Texas	USA
Casiano Floristán	Madrid	Spain
Sean Freyne	Dublin	Ireland
Claude Geffré OP	Paris	France
Norbert Greinacher	Tübingen	West Germany
Gustavo Gutiérrez	Lima	Peru
Herman Häring	Nijmegen	The Netherlands
Bas van Iersel SMM	Nijmegen	The Netherlands
Jean-Pierre Jossua OP	Paris	France
Hans Küng	Tübingen	West Germany
Nicholas Lash	Cambridge	Great Britain
Mary Mananzan OSB	Manila	Philippines
Norbert Mette	Münster	West Germany
Johann-Baptist Metz	Münster	West Germany
Dietmar Mieth	Tübingen	West Germany
Jürgen Moltmann	Tübingen	West Germany
Alphonse Ngindu Mushete	Kinshasa	Zaire
Aloysius Pieris SJ	Gonawala-Kelaniya	Sri Lanka
Jacques Pohier	Paris	France
David Power OMI	Washington, DC	USA
James Provost	Washington, DC	USA
Karl Rahner SJ+	Innsbruck	Austria
Giuseppe Ruggieri	Catania	Italy
Edward Schillebeeckx OP	Nijmegen	The Netherlands
Elisabeth Schüssler Fiorenza	Cambridge, Ma.	USA
David Tracy	Chicago, Ill.	USA
Knut Walf	Nijmegen	The Netherlands
Anton Weiler	Nijmegen	The Netherlands
Christos Yannaras	Athens	Greece

General Secretariat: Prins Bernhardstraat 2, 6521 AB Nijmegen, The Netherlands

Concilium 196 (2/1988): Ecumenism

CONCILIUM

List of Members

Advisory Committee: Spirituality

Directors:
Christian Duquoc, OP	Lyon	France
Casiano Floristán	Madrid	Spain

Members:
Frei Betto	São Paulo SP	Brazil
Enzo Bianchi	Magnano	Italy
Carlo Carozzo	Genova	Italy
Johannes van Galen OCarm	Aalsmeer	The Netherlands
Michel de Goedt OCD	Paris	France
Gustavo Gutiérrez	Lima	Peru
Ernest Larkin OCarm	Chicago/Ill.	USA
Jean Leclercq OSB	Clervaux	Luxembourg
Pierre de Locht	Brussels	Belgium
Edward Malatesta SI	Hsinchuang	Taïwan
Maria Martinell	Barcelona	Spain
Jan Peters OCD	Geysteren	The Netherlands
Samuel Rayan SI	Delhi	India
Samuel Ruiz	Chiapas	Mexico
Jean-Claude Sagne OP	Lyon	France
Charles Schleck CSC	Rome	Italy
Theodor Schneider	Armsheim	West Germany
Pedro Trigo	Caracas	Venezuela
Fernando Urbina	Madrid	Spain

CHRISTIAN IDENTITY

Edited by
Christian Duquoc
and
Casiano Floristán

English Language Editor
James Aitken Gardiner

T. & T. CLARK LTD
Edinburgh

Copyright © 1988, by Stichting Concilium and T. & T. Clark Ltd
All rights reserved. Nothing contained in this publication shall be multiplied and/or made public by means of print, photographic print, microfilm, or in any other manner without the previous written consent of Stichting Concilium, Prins Bernhardstraat 2, 6521 AB Nijmegen, Holland; and T. & T. Clark Ltd, 59 George Street, Edinburgh, Scotland.

April 1988
T. & T. Clark Ltd, 59 George Street, Edinburgh EH2 2LQ
ISBN: 0 567 30076 5

ISSN: 0010-5236

Typeset by C. R. Barber & Partners (Highlands) Ltd, Fort William
Printed by Page Brothers (Norwich) Ltd

Concilium: Published February, April, June, August, October, December. Subscriptions 1988: UK: £27.50 (including postage and packing); USA: US$49.95 (including air mail postage and packing); Canada: Canadian$59.95 (including air mail postage and packing); other countries: £27.50 (including postage and packing).

CONTENTS

Concilium 196 Special Column

The Future with Aids—a Challenge
  DIETMAR MIETH   xi

CHRISTIAN IDENTITY

Editorial
  CHRISTIAN DUQUOC
  CASIANO FLORISTÁN   xix

Part I
The Problem

The Self-identification Process
  THIERRY de SAUSSAUR   3

Christian Identity: Between Objectivity and Subjectivity
  PIERRE BÜHLER   17

Part II
In the View of Others

An Unbeliever's View of Christian Identity
  FRANÇOIS CHAVANNES   31

Transformation in Buddhism in Comparison with Platonic and Christian Notions
  MASAO ABE   41

Did God Make Anything Happen in Christianity? An Attempt at a Jewish Theology of Christianity
  SCHALOM BEN-CHORIN   61

Part III
Christian Identity and Community Membership

The Figure of Jesus in African Theology
   ALPHONSE NGINDU MUSHETE   73

The Burning Bush: Holy Scripture and the Reformation
Question of Identity
   PETER EICHER   80

The Part Played by Christ and the Spirit in the
Identification Process
   ISABELLE CHAREIRE   93

Part IV
Identity and Verification

The Limits of Personal and Communal Ethics
   PIERRE de LOCHT   107

Church Membership and Christian Identification
   CHRISTIAN DUQUOC   116

Part V

Conclusion: in the Interrogative
   CHRISTIAN DUQUOC   131

Contributors   134

CONCILIUM 196 Special Column

Dietmar Mieth

The Future with Aids—a Challenge

IT SEEMS as if we shall have to prepare ourselves for living with AIDS—the Auto Immune Deficiency Syndrome. The adaptability of the HIV-virus makes the scientific solving of the problem—already difficult—even more so. Consternation varies: reactions range from resistance to fatalism; debate rages on the socially responsible measures to be taken. One thing is however clear: the world looks different with AIDS; AIDS influences our view of the world; it challenges our thinking, our experience and our actions—challenges which we cannot escape. For that reason there are three questions which we must face up to: the question of meaning, the question of responsibility in health and politics, and the question of sexual behaviour.

1. THE QUESTION OF MEANING OR THE RELIGIOUS QUESTION

Many of the first ecclesiastical reactions have introduced the religious dimension direct. Statements by cardinals in which AIDS is described as 'God's scourge' or 'nature's resistance' can—in the effect they have—only be retracted with difficulty, even if and when subtly differentiated. They seem to take one thing for granted: the possibility that we can say authentically within our complex reality where God intervenes and what 'nature' is.

Objections can be raised to this way of thinking. For one thing, it is important for a religious answer to the challenge of AIDS not to ignore scientific explanation. It is true that the origin of AIDS cannot be explained in terms of an unbroken chain of cause and effect. But can we make 'God' or 'nature' into stopgaps of research? If we do, then suspicion of 'projection' will rise again out of the dusty past of religious criticism. The Christian God reveals himself in his history with man, he is no 'stopgap' in a system of explaining the world. The

Christian view of God does not begin with the assumption (cf. John 9:1–4) that God shows himself in an illness as the link between guilt and punishment. Let us remember Abraham's debate over God's judgment (cf. Genesis 18, 20–33). God's justice cannot arbitrarily strike the innocent as well. Is there anyone who doubts that AIDS can infect haemophiliacs, faithful married partners, and children?

But in AIDS is 'nature' defending itself? To say that, one would have to be able to point to where one can find (say in Africa) un-nature—in civilisation or in tradition? Does the HIV-virus itself represent a piece of unspoiled nature? The word 'nature' does not have much power to explain things here. If however the word 'nature' is used as a religious pictogram then it is accorded a mythical dimension.

Time and again one comes across people who bring up the theory of so-called historical decline in explanation. Above all they like using the pattern of a moral decline which, they say, shows up the collapse of the dominant forces of an epoch. But this view of history comes from the glorification of the development of nationalistic forces in military might and organisational skill; it cannot, for example, explain the vitality of the spirit in so-called periods of decline. In this connection one must draw attention to the fact that the observation of sexuality run wild, presupposed here, often includes only superficial phenomena; and that it represents for our time a questionable diagnosis, because AIDS increases suffering in the southern hemisphere much more than in the post-industrial culture. Furthermore, the contemporary swing of the pendulum in favour of a new impetus towards the sublimation of sexuality after a phase of de-sublimation of physicality can be identified before AIDS and not just after it.

If AIDS represents a challenge to our view of the world and to the religious questions bound up with it, then this challenge cannot be answered with such foreshortenings of perspective which are moreover not without cynicism towards the victims of the disease. Dealings with these victims clearly show that the religious question arises. Often it arises as a personal theodicy question or, generally, as a question to the God who permits irreversible suffering. It is however precisely our religious rationalisations in our explanation of the world which are wrecked by the theodicy question—this 'rock of atheism', as the German writer Martin Walser puts it. God answering Job demonstrates here the impossibility of the creature in his contingency reaching a clarification of this question (cf. Job 38ff). The only thing we know in Christian belief is that what God provides is not an answer of explanation but one of solidarity: in the Cross of Jesus Christ. From a Christian viewpoint, the aetiology of suffering takes second place to solidarity with those who suffer.

AIDS seems to provoke the religious question most strongly when it is a matter of the rivalry between belief and 'belief'. Fundamentally we as believers within western culture are continually believers in a double sense: on the one hand we acknowledge the creative power of God and our contingency as finite created beings—on the other hand we believe out of habit in the power of man to solve his problems and to break through, time and again, to new solutions to his problems. AIDS, in this respect, strengthens the experience that 'belief' in our technological culture carries in itself elements of idolatry. Certainly our religious scepticism should not impede research and technology for humane ends using humane means. It is no argument against our responsibility; but it limits the euphoria of our problem-solving mentality and teaches us a 'sober control of enthusiasm' (Goethe) in the face of so-called progress.

2. COMPANIONSHIP FOR THE SUFFERERS

The ill and suffering person is moved by three questions: why is it happening to me? What chances do I have? How can I live through the phase of illness, suffering and dying in a dignified manner?

An irreversible process of suffering and dying makes especial demands on the skills of self-acceptance, communication and help as companionship. In particular, it is a question of how far one can find constructive aspects in the suffering. Possible learning processes in suffering must however not be demanded *or cynically* laid claim to.

If, through ecclesiastical initiatives, special nursing homes for AIDS sufferers are set up or if this possibility is extended with state support—Mother Teresa has founded appropriate wards in the USA—then renewed consideration must also be given to 'Christian compassion'. If this is to be evidence of the proclamation of divine pity, then it has to be guided by Jesus' conduct which never in an individual case seeks to find guilt, which leaves the diagnosis up to the victim and grants them hope. Pity, in the sense of condescension is not the point here, but rather pity in the sense of the acceptance of a damaged life, pity which restores dignity to the person who has lost it.

Targets for our commitment should be: abolishing the isolation *of suffering; facilitating* self-determination; *lessening the pressure of* 'feeling a burden *to others';* making dying intelligible *as an integral process of living; incorporating the meaninglessness of early suffering and dying into the perception that life lived to the fulness of time still does not make a* full *life; testifying that life 'before God' gains an approval going beyond any values determined by human beings. One should testify to the basis of Christian hope, where there is a possibility of doing so and when people ask about it from within themselves, by reminding them of Christ's solidarity on the Cross and his admission through God to a new life.*

In every case the situation of AIDS patients should not be excluded from these general principles of companionship. The churches are faced here with a new task for which they should gather experiences and arrange for training.

The religious question unfolded at the outset links the questions 'what can we know?' and 'what should we do?' with the question 'what can we hope for?' (I. Kant). It does not spare us from research and action, but it also challenges us to set markers to show that believers have grounds for hope—and can live from that hope.

3. PROBLEMS OF ETHICAL RESPONSIBILITY FOR THE PROTECTION OF HEALTH

The rules of ethical responsibility which we apply to the danger of AIDS are not new. On the one hand it is a question of responsibility towards one's own life, on the other hand that of social responsibility according to the golden rule— never do anything to anyone that you would not wish to be done to you. Finally it is a question of the state's duties to protect against dangers, duties which have to be weighed up with competing rights and whose means have to be checked for their efficiency. Individual possibilities of responsibility lie either in a change in behaviour (in respect to e.g. drug-taking, sexuality) or in taking prophylactic measures where a change in behaviour fails because one cannot or will not change. The state cannot count on an individual change in behaviour, and must therefore push forward with enlightenment and prophylaxis, provided social standards are maintained. Devices which guarantee only relative security, as for example condoms, also belong in this area. There is a lot of talk of Roman Catholics having problems with such devices. But the condom would, according to Humanae Vitae (15), if used within the marriage for the protection of the healthy partner, be included among therapeutic devices i.e. among actions with a double effect in which birth control is not the intention. Moreover, on a pastoral level, the question has always been asked as to what, within a particular behavioural act which in itself is not deemed morally correct, is possible or even necessary to protect life.

The state has no alternative but to protect health, where, in extreme cases, it cannot count on the understanding of those infected (where indeed AIDS is perhaps used as a weapon). But there are reasons for the state to weigh up its power. These reasons are: that understanding is not brought about by using that power; that those who are 'healthy' bear a responsibility too; that rights of the personality are affected; that the efficiency of compulsory measures is uncertain; that tendencies towards discrimination are increased. Also relevant to a state under the rule of law is the avoidance of any downward slide towards discrimination.

Ecclesiastical exhortations to be responsible must also be more subtly differentiated. An example of this is the declaration of the Swiss National Commission entitled Justitia et Pax, *'on ethical questions concerning the AIDS disease' (9 November 1987). Assuming diverse phenomena, the dignity of the victims and the various areas of competence, it is up to the churches to increase understanding and offer their companionship. This also applies when AIDS is a reason for thinking again about the question of human sexual behaviour.*

4. AIDS AND SEXUALITY

The question of ethically right/wrong sexual behaviour is already decided in advance if judgment is passed on some forms of sexual behaviour responsible for spreading AIDS. The danger of AIDS is neither a necessary nor sufficient argument for establishing correct sexual behaviour. Questions of normative logic apart, it would be unwise to construct an argument which could be rendered null and void by a vaccine.

True, the question remains as to how far AIDS can be a more or less welcome kind of sexual-ethical exhortation (paraenesis) making people aware of or impressing on them that which is already recognised as right or wrong. This exhortation has the effect of saying something to the person who does indeed have the relevant knowledge but is not acting in accordance with that knowledge. What it says to that person is: 'Go ahead and do what you think is right anyway'. Here it is a matter of a back-up argument for the knowledge of the consequence of that, namely that knowledge and action are falling apart. The question of giving reasons for the responsibility attached to what is right is not affected by AIDS. Another question to be borne in mind is the psychological meaning of the danger of AIDS for the social acceptance of stricter sexual norms, in so far as people do not often make decisions about their conduct out of moral self-obligation.

Also, as far as the much discussed relationship between homosexuality and AIDS is concerned, there is no single new argument in the question of whether homosexual actions are morally right or not. True, we have to take account of developments in the internal ethos of the victims in the same way as with other endangered groups.

The danger of AIDS is a cause for and a catalyst of thoughts on values like restraint, love and faithfulness. But these thoughts also originated before the danger of AIDS arose. The crisis of the expectations placed on sexual libertarianism is the moment of experience. Some observations point to the fact that the pressure to conform—triggered by sexual promises—is decreasing. Physical relations are taken more seriously; they demand discussion and care. The minimal principle that injury should be prevented in erotic encounters may indeed receive new impetus through AIDS, but the signs are growing that people are thinking more constructively about their sexuality. The prophets of early sexuality and promiscuity are becoming more careful. Whoever wishes to practise restraint is not put under pressure or isolated. Periods of time between first meetings and sexual contacts are lengthening. There are longer spells of practice with patience ... ethics, if they are correct, are also open to experience. In this connection it ought also to be seen that the development towards non-married long-term relationships is less of an alternative to marriage *than an* alternative to promiscuity.

All this is not primarily connected with the fears that AIDS triggers. Rather it seems that experience is being imparted through the more open dealings between the generations and between groups of young people, and it seems that ethically relevant perceptions of values such as restraint, love and faithfulness are being clarified in terms of their human justice. *There is more demand for the 'emotional expanses' of love than for sexual sensations.*

The problems of ecclesiastical sexual ethics are of course not solved by that. But they can be discussed in another associated area. Nor are the problems of the so-called 'risk groups' thereby diminished. Often they are also 'risk groups' just because their opportunities for gaining experience and the actual experiences they have undergone are different. They are called upon to discuss again with one another their experiences and perceptions in a responsible way; and they must be given room for that purpose in the Church too.

Translated by Gordon Wood

Note that this Special Column, like others in this series, is written under the sole responsibility of the author.

CHRISTIAN IDENTITY

Editorial

THIS ISSUE of 'Concilium' is concerned with Christian identity. We have chosen this subject because Christians are uncertain about their identity. They tend to reject self-affirmation through group membership, for all it seems to do is culturally to efface the very particularity which they are looking for. That, however, is not the ultimate reason for their indecision. It stems more from the individualism affecting the western democracies. John Paul II reminded American Catholics that theirs was not a self-service Church in which each person could choose what was to his or her taste and leave aside what was found wanting. This is not an easy problem. Should one opt for perfect integration in a group with a structure, ideology and dynamics which decide what one is; or should one opt for self-definition, only to risk uncertainty about what enables one to say one is a Christian anyway? That is the setting of the articles in this issue.

First, on premises drawn from psychology, we had to define the concept of an identification process. T. de Saussure has provided this intellectually respectable basis for the various studies.

The process of identification is also the means by which a group acquires a consciousness of self, both as self-awareness and as awareness of its relations to the outside world. Recent history shows that indecision in this respect affects not only individual Christians but the churches. And their criteria for identification have gone awry. Pierre Bühler describes this development as experienced recently by Reformed churches.

The process by which one defines one's own identity is visible to others. Acknowledgment by others is an essential aspect of that process. We decided on three views from the outside: the unbeliever's, the Buddhist's, and the Jew's. Unfortunately several authors approached for the first of the three did not submit articles, so we asked a Camus specialist to describe his author's notion of Christianity. A Buddhist and a Jew have offered their own views.

To define the concept, examine the history and provide outside perceptions it was necessary to reveal the structural elements of identity. This has been done in respect of three topics: Jesus; Scripture; and Christ and the Spirit. Ngindu, Eicher and Chareire have tackled them in that order. We also thought it necessary to describe the ethical consequences and Fr de Locht undertook this task. I (C. Duquoc) have provided an article on Christian belonging and an account of provisional conclusions.

We are sure that readers will discover omissions and imprecisions, but we are also convinced that these articles will make possible an honest evaluation of a difficult question.

Translated by J. G. Cumming

Christian Duquoc OP
Casiano Floristán

PART I

The Problem

Thierry de Saussure

The Self-identification Process

IT WOULD be quite illusory to think that human beings are born, develop and find themselves on the basis of their genetic programming and personal capacities of autonomous behaviour.[1] Both within themselves and in their unavoidable relationships with their surroundings, an increasingly complex network develops in which the whole gamut of their experiences circulates: uniting or opposing, unifying or separating the thousands of images from inside or outside which, born of their wishes and fears, take shape and form their psychic life.

Section Two will outline the beautiful and tragic story of how each of us, born to life, tries to be born to himself or herself and to grow as a person in willed relation to others. A growing process, nevertheless, which we all know will end in death, a death hinted at in each stage of growth by our successive discoveries of what we are not, by comparison with what we dream of being.

First we need to define some psychological, and more particularly psychoanalytical terms, developed gradually through processes of observation and discovery, in order to give a more accurate account of this delicate process of self-identification.[2]

1. A LITTLE TERMINOLOGY

'Identification' is a term whose very ambiguity is a good reflection of the process of coming and going by which we develop ourselves in relation to others. Identifying can mean recognising an object (including oneself) through its characteristics (its identity card, as it were), but can also (particularly with the addition of the reflexive pronoun) represent the psychological process by which, according to Laplanche and Pontalis, 'a subject assimilates an aspect, property, attribute of others and transforms himself, wholly or in part, by modelling himself on others. Personality is formed and differentiated by a series of identifications.' Identification is made up of sympathy, more or less conscious imitation, empathy, mental contagion, deluding projection. It can be 'heteropathic', identifying one's own person with another, or 'idiopathic', as in the case of ego-centricity. The two types together contribute to the formation of 'us', the group, the crowd, our whole civilization even.

In his studies of *adaptation*, Piaget has shown this to be based on two psychic processes: *accommodation* (modification of the subject in the direction of the object: 'the habit makes the monk'!) and *assimilation* (modification of the object by the subject: the apple one eats).

In psychoanalysis, we need to make the distinction between identification, which, in contact with a model, favours the development of certain characteristics likely to germinate in the subject already, and 'incorporation' and 'introjection'.

Incorporation is a very primitive process, operative above all in the first year of life, by which a baby 'in a more or less phantasmal manner, pushes an object into and keeps it in its body ... it forms the bodily prototype of introjection and identification' (*op. cit.* Note 1). So, for example, the suckling infant not only incorporates its mother's milk, but also parts of her, as it were.

Introjection is one of the defence mechanisms. Close to incorporation and identification, it also consists in making the qualities of an object pass phantasmally from outside to inside, but without this being basically a bodily movement. It can deal in ideas, convictions, feelings. Its defensive aspect lies in the fact that the subject is thereby appropriating characteristics of others that may be completely strange to him or her, and is trying through this process to diminish the agonising distance of otherness. An example would be an individual feeling alienated from a homogenous group and therefore adopting its accent, its types of reaction, its customs.

The opposite of introjection is *projection*, equally a defence mechanism and for the same reasons, by which the subject attributes to others, unconsciously, thoughts or feelings which are in fact his or her own, but which he or she cannot, for the moment or ever, accept as such.

The *Ego* is one of the three elements of the second theory in which Freud described the psychic framework and its mode of functioning. The other two are the *Id* (the reserve of bio-psychic drives) and the *Superego*, of which more later. If, by definition, unconscious defence mechanisms belong in the Ego along with the subconscious, the Ego contains the only conscious part of a person. The Ego, with its conscious, subconscious and unconscious zones, is taxed with finding solutions to the conflict between the pressure of drives from the Id in anarchic quest of their satisfactions and the demands of external reality: space, time, other people, social constraints and so on.

As for the *Self*, it could be defined as the overall perception people make and remake of their persons completed and defined by their sexed bodies. The Self is in a way the place where the Ego is incarnated in the *soma*.

2. HOW EVERYTHING (OR NOTHING) BECOMES 'I', THEN 'SELF'

This section will try to give a broad outline of the main relational movements by which a person is born to him or her self in quest of identity.

(a) From one Birth to Another

We should remember that, by comparison with the other mammals, the human infant is born very prematurely, particularly as regards its nervous system. This means a lasting and complete dependence dating from physical birth; it determines the alternation of joy and existential security with distress and agonised anger that dominates early life, according to the presence or absence of the person who mainly looks after the infant, usually the mother who has carried it in her womb.

The numerous observations made of the first months of life, the analyses of dreams and fantasies conserved in the child's unconscious and even into adulthood, show irrefutably that at the outset of their lives, human beings are bathed in an 'oceanic' feeling. Not recognising their finiteness, their existence apart from their mother, they experience the sensation of being everything and self-sufficient. This gives rise to the illusion of omnipotence which, when reality imposes regret for its loss, remains throughout life as a wish in the unconscious.

Day after day, the alternating experience of the presence of its mother and of wellbeing, then of her absence and frustration, compels a baby to learn a harsh reality: that of its own separate, limited, dependent existence, subject to time and space. During the second month of life, seeing itself looked at by its mother's eyes, it begins to feel that it exists and to open up to what will become the subject-object relationship. The feeling of 'I', separate from 'not I', through the distinction between areas of skin, is outlined. The joy in this discovery is shown by the first smiles in response to the smiles of the henceforth loved-one, the prototypes of mirror behaviour that will progressively orientate the baby's image of its body.

There is joy, certainly, which will be a powerful stimulus to wanting to be, throughout its life, the appetite and relational necessity of its 'I' to another; but there is also a basic distress, as it inevitably experiences loneliness in the absence of the person on whom its survival depends.

The repeated experience of contact and non-contact with its mother's body, with their before, during and after, inserts the infant in time and space. Gradually, it will come to imagine the loved face and body even in their absence and will find in auto-eroticism (thumb-sucking, touching its own body, pleasure in movement) palliatives for its isolation. This is the basis of the narcissism to come, the capacity for loving oneself, which is both essential for survival and necessary for loving others, by identification.

Acceptance of separateness is painful and we all seek for a compensatory fusion all our lives, even if only unconsciously. This loss of the 'oceanic' feeling of totality is so tragic that it led one of my patients, a severely disturbed adult to say: 'Basically, there is nothing between birth and death'. (He had, incidentally, tried to recapture the feeling of 'everything', of 'paradise' which he could not bear having to lose, in religion. While this produced certain joys of a mystic bent, it also forced him to realise that, unlike the 'true' mystics—who were also men and women of action—these joys were merely avoidance of daily life and relationships he could not bear: just like the Gospels, which stress incarnation, the historical aspect, relationship to God and other human beings in their otherness.)

As the baby's 'I' develops, it discovers it is hungry. Hungry for milk, for contact, for care and love. The tragic and inevitable frustrations of these appetites produce its earliest deep aggressive impulses. These give rise to phantasms in which the image of its mother is split into 'good' and 'bad' with the whole gamut of ambivalent experiences symbolised so well in fairy stories—Little Red Riding-Hood, Tom Thumb, Hansel and Gretel. ... Through the process of *incorporation*, the infant fantasises that it is devouring, so destroying its mother, and that she, as its mirror-image, might do the same to it—hence the myths of ogres and common catch-phrases such as 'You're good enough to eat'. We shall return to the play of this ambivalence—love/hate, desire/destroy—in the section dealing with the paradoxes of identity.

It is not till between its sixth and ninth month that a baby completes its mirror perception of its absolute separation from its mother and of the limits of its own body and hers. This is really the true psychic birth of the subject. It will then experience terrible anxieties and depressive phrases which can be overcome by the joy of feeling itself being and becoming. Anxiety will also come from having to distinguish its mother from other relations and from 'strangers' who, for a time, frighten it.

(b) From 'I' to Other and the Ego

During the second and third years, the feeling of 'I' separate from the Other will develop into a powerful discovery of the Ego. Its neurological development will enable the child to walk and talk, through which it can express its pleasure in its growing autonomy through being able to run away and say 'No', and its desire for company and communication in new ties. Imitation of and identification with people around it play a primordial part in these processes.

Being able, however tiny it may be, to make other members of the family run to it, to provoke their smiles and admiration or their anger and reprobation merely by crying, by throwing a mug on the floor, by producing the first stool in the right place and at the right time, by picking and holding out a flower, renews the child's feeling of omnipotence for a time and contributes to inscribing this omnipotence as an undying wish in its subconscious. (Think how many subtle or obvious ways adults still find to satisfy their quest for omnipotence and desire to manipulate others!)

Putting building blocks on top of one another and then knocking the tower over, making sandcastles, tasting everything, dirtying and cleaning oneself, hitting and stroking, naming people and things, trying out new words: all these, among thousands of things it does every day, are ways in which the child discovers its power over the world, always looking to gauge adult reaction as it does so. And when, using the same pencil and the same hand, it can arouse admiration for 'drawing' on a sheet of paper and provoke a scolding for 'scribbling' on the new wallpaper in its room, what a basic discovery: 'good' and 'bad' are no longer separated on the Manichean principle; the same being is capable of the best actions and the worst. Not only the child, but its parents, which it begins to see as limited, sometimes making mistakes, incapable of magically saving it from hurt, and capable of not knowing what it is thinking or imagining in wishes and fears.

One can easily see how far the child's Ego is developed at this stage, in which it is always trying to find adaptive compromises between the limitless pressures of the drives of the Id and the demands of the reality which it keeps encountering in its harshness, richness and multiple nuances.

(c) Towards the Sexed Self

Close observation will show that girls and boys in their second year already demonstrate attitudes specific to their sex and as differentiated in their response to other members of the same or the opposite sex. Yet it is not for another year or two that they begin to investigate with curiosity and pleasure the parts of their bodies that mark out their sex, at the same time as they attribute different sexes to those around them.

This is a new feeling of limitation in relation to the phantasms of omnipotence and totality which, in this sphere, underlie the myth of the androgyne. But it is a determining factor in defining identity, particularly when this real advance is made through good identification with the parent or close relations of the same sex who have harmoniously integrated their sexuality.

This first phase of sexual identity is shot through, for both girls and boys, by fear of castration. Little girls fear they are missing something, have had something cut off, while the boys, who think they have something extra, are afraid, like all who have more than others, that this will be taken away from them. This perceptual error tends in some people to be combined with a confusion between *having* or not having (a vital matter at that age ... and all their lives, in many cases) and *being*, and it is especially in this error that there takes root phallocratism, a badly-assimilated sort of feminism and their harmful abuse.

Castration anxiety is normally overcome through the child's progressive understanding that girls as well as boys have a definite sex and that the vaginal cavity is just as much a source of pleasure and procreation as the penis. If these positive discoveries do not take place in childhood, or are not confirmed at puberty, sexual identity will be compromised, showing characteristics such as passivity, inhibition, shame and envy.

First experienced on the physical level, these castration-fantasies, which Freud at first thought came from clumsy, guilt-provoking teaching, have now been shown not only to be universal, but also to mark a decisive and formative turning-point for every individual. Unless a child regresses into the fear it felt at this period and so becomes pathologically fixated on earlier stages of development, this transitory phase will provide it with access to what is perhaps the most formative contribution to the construction of identity: the discovery of 'like' and 'different', of 'same' and 'other'. This is 'symbolic castration', the definitive integration of limitation.

A basic characteristic of the dawning Oedipal period is that all relationships will henceforth be experienced within the triangle: 'I am like, I am different from'. A deep differentiation becomes operative at this stage, as in love: loving those who are like you (in sex, character, occupation and so on) favours, through identification, maturation of your identity by developing common specificities. It is sometimes also a source of more coalescing satisfactions (soul-sisters), but equally of attendant anxieties (of absorbing the other or disappearing into the other). Loving those who are different from you means rejoicing in complementarity and experiencing what you are not through the other. But it can lead to anxiety over too great an otherness, a recurrence of the 'fear of strangers' dormant in us all from the end of our first year of life.

(d) Friend or Foe of Identity: the Superego

This third component of the psyche comes to the help of the Ego by working in the subconscious from the age of four to six, so as to spare the conscious zones from apparently intolerable pressures arising from the incompatibility between the limitless demands of the drives of the Id and the evidence of reality, now better understood and filtered through education. The Superego, a sort of infantile pre-morality, ultimately destined to be relieved as far as possible by a thinking and evolving ethic, allows the child to socialise. The kernel of the Superego is very subjective and deals in individual psychic economy, in what the subject has, rightly or wrongly, repressed as being, in his or her mind, unacceptable behaviour. But this kernel is wrapped, as in the layers of an onion, in explicit injunctions from teachers and the implicit influence of the parents' Superegos, with an outer skin of group and class practices, behaviour proper to a culture or civilisation. The Superego develops through a massive repression of these multiple injunctions which limit the play of drives, till now relatively free and controlled from outside by the child's family circle, in order to ensure a more or less happy outcome of the Oedipus phase and what is from now on marked by virtually complete amnesia of early infancy.

The Superego, however, is more than just repression; it is also the 'interiorisation' of the child's loving parents who protect it from unbearable, not to say death-dealing experiences. And then it contains elements which are very important for self-identification, the *Ideals*: the *ideal Ego*, made up of early images drawn from representations made by the infant of its idealised parents, whom it would so much like to resemble when it grows up. This is the source of the dreams of greatness we all carry. And the *Ideal of the Ego*, what the child thinks it ought to be in order to correspond to the overall expectations of its parents; this is the root of future fears of 'what people will say'.

So one can see that the Superego with its Ideals plays a considerable role in the unconscious, sometimes by stimulating and guiding the growth of the Ego, sometimes in conflict with the Ego through its limiting and repressive promptings, or because it imposes rules on the child that are not necessarily its own. These expectations and demands are the more constraining to the child in that, during the formation of the Superego, it is still completely dependent on parental love, which it thinks it can win or lose by bargaining, as it were, its behaviour for it.

Unconscious, the Superego remains primordial and infantile in individuals in all sectors that have not been made available to conscious access during growth by an ethic progressively based on free, personal choices. While conscious ideals are stimulating as ultimate references which one knows one can never attain, the Ideals of the unconscious can be a source of paralysis, a burden of generalised and continual guilt-feelings, even leading to depression, because of their absolute nature.[3]

(e) Beyond Infancy

If the basic components of our pyschic make-up and its operation are acquired by the age of six, it is clear that all later individual development, if it is healthy and consists of acquisitions of understanding proper to maturity, will bring modifications and adjustments necessary to the growth of the Ego and the integration of the Self.

Thanks mainly to the acquisition of the Superego and the relative calming of the conflicts of drives it brings, the *latency* period (six to twelve) and its characteristic socialisation furnish the child with numerous sources of identification. Other families, school, gangs and their leaders, all offer models differing from and complementing the basic model provided by its parents. The child's whole spirit of curiosity and psychic energy are then directed to discovering interests and satisfactions through friendships, social contacts, science, religion, sport, artistic endeavours, and so on.

At this age children identify strongly with groups, thereby developing behaviour patterns that were previously only embryonic. This is when the 'collective personality' takes wing, when different 'we's' are discovered, known persons or strangers, sources of comfort or fear. In return, they undergo trial by collective opinion, acceptance and rejection, elements that lead them either to doubt or to reinforce their identity, which they can now define to a greater extent.

Next come the great shocks of puberty and adolescence, unfortunately often bundled together in our civilization. *Puberty* revives the Oedipus conflicts; *adolescence* should, like latency, with its huge range of new acquisitions, enable these to be reassessed and re-evaluated in their social and cultural setting.[4] The violent somatic and physiological changes of this period shake identity and identifications to their roots. The sexed self is now evident and adolescents waver between their desire to show this off or hide it, now overcoming, now succumbing to their doubts. Each advance, each retreat, any sort of a-typicality in relation to the peer group, takes on catastrophic proportions. The Ego's (unconscious) defence mechanisms are either set back, or else intensified to an excessive degree, as in projection, annihilation, idealisation ... in order to combat the agony stemming from the disharmony between an adult body, an often still infantile affectivity, and social constraints.

But adolescents have an inkling that they will soon no longer be able to avoid internalising the conflict between their unbounded appetites and drives and the Ideals and constraints (unconscious, from the Superego) which they still try to project on to the adults who surround them. This is the terrible conflict of realisations through which the conscious zones of the Ego have to find the compromises needed for a healthy adaptation, without which mental illness threatens.

Their parents, their basic models for identification, become, due to a recurrence of Oedipal conflicts, the occasion for unbearable over-excitations of libido and aggressivity; young people want to run away from them, to reject them as principal models and central source of security. Not yet being able to find this in themselves, they are torn between introspection and the search for self-identity, and escapism, throwing themselves on anyone or any group that seems to offer new identifications. Caught between despairing longing for the objects and relationships of their childhood and their enthusiasm for substitutional models, their incoherence is equalled only by their anxiety. All too often, what they try to identify with brings only introjections, a sort of defensive imitations: these do not develop much in themselves, but shield them from the loss or excessive pressure of the internal images formed through contact with the parents they are now trying to de-idealise.

Immediately taking on the 'protective colouring' of each new group environment, like chameleons, they can lose their guiding thread when confronted with a meeting between their close relatives and their varied centrifugal relationships. This is why they try to keep the two groups apart at any price.

We know how important young people find groups of their own age. But it can also be dangerous for them to use these groups to fix their vocations on such scattered identities, particularly when the underlying ideal is not very solidly anchored in reality.[5] Some young people cultivate fanaticism and heroism, even to the extent of putting death forward as an ideal, perhaps symbolising the primitive symbiosis as a refuge in the face of threats of disintegration of their identity or as a paradoxical conjuration.

Their often turbulent conflict with their external environment is primarily, as we have seen, an inner conflict in which identity and identifications seek new forms as a result of the upheavals wrought by somatic changes on the Self. The homophilia of this age helps girls and boys to consolidate their sexed identity till the moment when they feel strong enough to face the opposite sex in its difference. Just as in the beginning of the Oedipal phase, the infant is torn, on the one hand, between admiration and love for the parent of the same sex, by identification, and, on the other, attraction to the other in the first heterosexual stirrings. Each time, the opposite sex is the target of aggressivity, as one can see in the playgrounds of mixed schools.

I will not dwell here on the later stages of the evolution of identity and self-identification, from the developmental point of view, since the last section deals with the paradoxes of those that persist through adult life. Two points, however, need mentioning:

(i) The maturation period of from twenty to thirty is just as influential for identity and self-acceptace. As long as one is an apprentice or student, identifications, development of the Ego, self-perception are clearly important. But it is one thing to be on the threshold of adult life with the full freedom and sometimes the compulsion to criticise those whose place one is anxious to occupy, and another to find oneself and experience oneself in an adult socio-professional situation. Here, one not only has to go on 'making oneself by making oneself' (Ajuriaguerra), but to feel the (often considerable) pressure of what others make of one in return, expect of one or reject in one—rightly or wrongly.

I am thinking of an 'inter-church' married couple, put forward as an ideal by so many other couples and institutions of an ecumenical bent, who used them as proof of the success of inter-church marriages. Caught in this situation and this role, this man and woman took more than ten years to face up to the serious conflict that had come about before their children were born and which led them in the end to an inevitable separation.

(ii) It also needs to be stressed that it is wrong to see adolescence as the great crisis *par excellence*. Seeing it like this may be due to a desire for easy reassurance in the face of the deep but less turbulent conflicts of infancy, or to protect oneself from those sometimes equally disturbing conflicts for identity and self-acceptance, such as pregnancy, professional setbacks, a mutilating operation, bereavement, divorce, the menopause or andropause, old age. All these are stages or events which can deeply shake identity through reshaping one's narcissistic or relational economy, with the joys and sorrows, expansions or retractions they bring with them.

3. PARADOXES OF IDENTITY

The matter, I fear, becomes yet more complicated and nuanced. From the preceding, it will have emerged that it would be illusory to view personal identity as the simple outcome of the growth of the Ego, once all the many external influences have been either accepted or rejected. Through the process of incorporations, identifications, introjections and defensive projections, it is deep in the subconscious that a person lives out the conflicts between self love and hate, love and hatred for his or her parents, then for all the other significant people who have polarised relationships throughout his or her development. These become 'internalised objects' and remain, even if actually dead, as living images in sometimes stormy dialogue with the unconscious Ego, stemming from the Superego, the demands and Ideals they have set up there. Acts of awareness alone allow one to free oneself here and there from these hoary visitors and so open oneself to new and personal choices.

Understanding dynamic identity in terms of these paradoxes allows one to steer clear of the two erroneous beliefs: in 'implacable fate' and in an idealised personal freedom. The latter is possible only in areas that have been the object of real acts of awareness, while the parts subject to determinism render the ideology of the 'authenticity' of the person illusory. Using this term in its current sense ignores the fact that human beings are not transparent to themselves, because of their unconscious and the many actors who play upon its stage.

To illustrate these paradoxes, let us go back to some of the landmarks in development mentioned in the previous section.

When a baby is born into the world, it is programmed not only genetically, but also temperamentally by its genitors. What its parents are going to find, over the years, is not a completely new being becoming 'himself' or 'herself'; from their own childhood they have build up in themselves, in the existing image of their own parents, scenarios that affect their offspring. They will therefore be active spectators of the personal combinations made by their child of its—unconscious—projects and theirs, through the inscription of important parts of their own Egos, Superegos and Ideals in the child's.

Pro-geniture: geniture for whom? However generous the parents are, they can hardly avoid hoping, more or less unconsciously, that their child will be child-for-them, the source of their narcissistic anxieties and satisfactions; in this way their demands will be built into its project.

When, as we have seen, the infant sucks at the breast of its mother, it incorporates parts of her it sees as good or bad as its phantasies dictate, with which it will live in love or aggression, desire or guilt, applied to them or to itself, in a dialogue that it will later repeat, through projections and displacements, in other relationships in its life.[6]

When the child later discovers that, like other people, it is both good and bad (Could there be a theological analogy here with Luther's '*simul peccator et justus*', opposed to our infantile sequence of 'perfect-sullied-sinner-purified'?) it is already faced with the inner conflict between the objects of its drives and what, rightly or wrongly, it imagines its parents expect of it.

At the Oedipal stage, the child's parents really become two for it, sending it different and sometimes conflicting messages. So a boy, for example, will hear: 'Be like your father', so as to become a man, and 'Don't be like your father', because only your father is allowed to desire your mother.

In adolescence, finally, pending leaving father and mother, young people enter into an intense conflict with their inner images of their parents. This conflict can be productive of so much anxiety that young people try to project it in systematic opposition to their surroundings. But their Superego and Ideals, formed in contact with those of their parents, are so interwoven, in their identity, with their own projects, that it is not uncommon for those who have been through the most turbulent adolescence to become most like their father or mother by the time they are thirty. The opposite also applies, in that those who have had the most tranquil adolescence become the more clearly differentiated adults.

So Hamlet's celebrated dilemma, 'To be or not to be, that is the question', raises itself at each stage: the whole question of one's identity in relation to others. Because it is a question of the impossible (evangelical) endeavour to love oneself and others in one non-contradictory movement. Guilt—and hence aggressivity—stems from the tension between one's self and one's ideal of oneself, while, as Freud says, when they coincide this always produces a feeling of triumph.

But this is rare and conflict persists. To the point where, when a person's own Superego and Ideals remain too subjected to those of his or her parents, it can lead to illness. This person then organises him- or herself into a 'false self', splitting into a personality 'for external use' and a crushed deep Ego, with no living way out.

The religious I mentioned earlier, for example, needed analysis to show him that his 'vocation' was in fact based purely on his mother's prohibition, passed a thousand times into his unconscious, on ever having any other women before her. A mother long since dead, but still exercising this prohibition, even though, while living, she had consciously and explicitly deplored the fact that he had never married.

It would have been appropriate, at the end of this article, to say something of the role of Ideals in relation to personality, of their possible adjustment or what happens when our public face obliges us to hide, to make ourselves good narcissistically, even to compensate for what we regret not being. But this is a wide subject that does not fit into the confines of this essay.

4. PSYCHOANALYTIC ANTHROPOLOGY AND CHRISTIANITY

A few questions to conclude.

Biblical anthropology sees human beings only in relation to the saving God. The psychoanalyst, naturally, pricks up his ears at this: what God? And when Christians talk of 'liberation through Jesus Christ', of 'new birth' or 'resurrection', what do they mean in relation to what psychoanalysis has discovered about human beings? Are they referring to a god projected by the Id, subject to limitless wish? A god whose religion would allow me, by mystic fusion or crushing enabling him to become all in me, to avoid the harsh loss of omnipotence? Or again to a god projected by the Superego, with its limiting demands and its persecuting, guilt-producing ideals? And would there be a God who, revealed in the humanity of Jesus Christ, could be encountered by the conscious zones of the Ego?

And in this hypothesis, would the 'new birth' be an abolition of human nature and the processes described above, for example?

Psychoanalysis teaches that only acts of self-realisation can release an individual from the trammels and tyrannies in which he inwardly imprisons himself, stifling from not being able truly to be and become, for fear of offending both his internalised Ideals and their external human sources and supports.

So perhaps 'liberation' through Jesus Christ and the perspective of the resurrection can mean something in the same line. In this case, the discovery by the Ego of God's revelation in Jesus (the true Son, the only man in whom being, word and action are never contradictory) would, far from abolishing human specificity, liberate men and women from their obsession with becoming the god fashioned by their own desires (the idol, the Fall: 'You will be like gods'). This discovery would open up the possibility of accepting their sinful condition, limited in time, space and the interdependence of relationships. Then, instructed both by the Word of God and the secular knowledge willed by God, in the knowledge of the inevitability of their conflictual nature 'from generation to generation', they would see themselves invited to take on this nature with good humour, in the hope of themselves becoming, thanks to God's loving looking on them, the only love which, according to faith, does not imprison but calls to being.

Translated by Paul Burns

Notes

1. The limited space of this article, the necessary generalisation of very complex problems which have been studied many times from many different psychological schools, as well as my identity as a Freudian psychoanalyst, have led me to approach this subject mainly in the light of the contributions made by Freud and his successors in this field.

For a more technical, scientific and complete treatment of the subject, see, *inter alia*, the excellent work by N. Duruz *Narcisse en quête de soi. Etude des concepts de narcissisme, de moi et de soi en psychanalyse et en psychologie* (Brussels 1985). Besides a good account of different psychoanalytic schools, he also describes non-psychoanalytic approaches to the question of the Ego and the self, such as the phenomenological, behavourist, socio-cognitive or systemic theories.

2. J. Laplanche and J. B. Pontalis, in their *Vocabulaire de la psychanalyse* ([8]Paris 1984), give more complete and rigorous definitions of both the analysis of the different meanings which the psychoanalytic concepts described below have acquired, and of other concepts on which this article depends.

3. On the subject of this absolutisation of the unconscious Ideals and their basic rejection, especially in adolescence, in favour of relative ideals and the abolition of the 'all or nothing' regime, including its functioning in the realm of Christian ethics, see the excellent little work by J. le Du *L'idéal en procés* (Paris 1975).

4. The re-workings of identity in the course of adolescence are vividly described by the psychoanalyst E. H. Erikson in his *Adolescence and Crisis: the Quest for Identity* and *Luther before Luther*.

5. On the subject of psychological maturation of the priestly vocation, see the articles by the psychiatrists and psychoanalysts A. Vergote, R. Querinjean, C. Darmstadter and T. de Saussure under the general heading 'Formation apostolique des prêtres' in *Le Supplément* 90 (Paris 1969).

6. On the procoious roots of the instincts of libido and aggression, see M. Klein and J. Rivière *L'amour et la haine* (Paris 1979).

Pierre Bühler

Christian Identity: Between Objectivity and Subjectivity

'For identity is never "fixed", never "complete" as a kind of framework of the personality would be, or anything which is static and permanent.'[1]

IDENTITY IS a fundamental component of spirituality. A truly spiritual life can only be lived by one who knows who he is and knows himself, accepts and comes to terms with himself as he is, who knows that he is at one with himself, in harmony with himself, and who knows that the strength and lasting nature of this identity will carry him through the vicissitudes of his existence. Man needs such a feeling, such an awareness of identity; without a more or less constituted and articulated identity, man feels lost, alienated, at odds with himself.

But this identity is at the same time a very fragile dimension, open and therefore exposed. In the twists of everyday life, man can lose his identity, and even if he does not lose it, he has never acquired it once and for all. It is the object of a ceaseless arduous quest whose stakes are life and death.

This exposed and difficult nature of the search for identity may be seen as one consequence, amongst others, of the modern condition. In fact, it may be said that the progressive development of modern times has thrown into prominence the problem of identity for modern man, casting him into what are commonly called 'identity crises', crises which give him cause both for concern and self-examination. The Christian does not escape this modern condition, and it is therefore from this point of departure that the problem of his Christian identity must be posed. Taken in this perspective, this problem proves to be created by an interplay of objectivity and subjectivity.

1. THE SEARCH FOR IDENTITY IN THE MODERN CONDITION

(a) The loss of impact of objective references

The question 'Who am I?', even if it concerns man at the most profound level of his being, does not however confine itself to a private sector, an internal secrecy within which man finds himself cut off from the outside world. The search for identity is carried out rather as a dynamic process placing man within the animate area of multiple interactions with everything surrounding him. Identity, considered as identification, is developed by the integration of the various aspects which make up the reality of man in a perspective of unity which gives them sense, consistency and form. This process whereby man identifies himself, understands himself and establishes himself in his concrete reality necessarily passes through outside mediations, identification models or references which present themselves to him and on which he can base his feeling of identity. These references are numerous, and everyone can, in his way, rely on them, giving them the respective weight which he wishes to give them. Among these references can be especially mentioned the various attachments: family, sex, class, nation, race, political party, church, profession; the ideological references: conception of the world, political conviction, religion; behavioural identification: lifestyle, moral attitude, religious practice; the roles to be adopted; wealth and possessions; work accomplished; career; posterity; etc. So, everyone finds his identity by placing himself within the framework of these different references, sorting them out and linking them together.

Now, if the search for identity has become such an arduous task in the present situation, it is precisely because in modern times, objective references of identification have lost the greater part of their impact. The revolution brought about in the feeling of life by modern phenomena—technical progress, industrialisation, mass civilisation—leaves man alone in his search for identity. Modern evolution leads to a complex, elusive world in which identification references, formerly so strong, become blurred and lose their structuring significance. The great models of thought collapse, the numerous attachments no longer truly give direction, and moral ideas become relative. At the same time, under the influence of excessive technological development, the areas of life experienced become occasions for alienation rather than self-realisation: production-line work, organised leisure, compartmentalised time, standardised housing, etc. But in this situation there is a paradoxical tension. In fact, the more man is left alone, the more his task is emphasised. In the absence of objective references, man himself becomes the subject responsible for his search for identity. The call is addressed to his subjectivity even though the latter is abandoned to itself, left without meaningful outside supports.

(b) Christian identity without objective references

Christian identity is no exception, it too is affected by the modern crisis. In fact, everything leads one to believe that with the effects of secularisation, of criticism of religion and of increasing religious indifference, believers have also lost the identification references which were traditionally before them. We will simply try to clarify this aspect briefly according to three different viewpoints.

(i) For a long time attachment to a church could be considered as an institutionally assured guarantee of Christian identity. Today, this attachment is a problem and no longer constitutes an undisputed reference of identity. The awareness of Christian identity no longer amounts to belonging to the Church. Even if this attachment can continue to be a part of it, it is not—as in the Christian State—its basic frame of reference.

(ii) In the same way, one could make the adherence to a more or less precise *body of doctrine* the distinctive sign of Christian identity: a Christian is one who holds as true the fundamental affirmations of the Christian faith. Here, too, such a procedure proves to be an unacceptable objectivisation. Intellectual assent does not amount to an awareness of identity, which turns on a deeper concord concerning life itself.

(iii) Finally, one could also traditionally see grounds for establishing Christian identity in *a certain type of moral behaviour, or practical attitude*: the Christian life finds its expression in the undertaking of a programme of charity, in the respect for a precise moral code. With the effects of modern secularisation, such an objective reference has also become invalid. Christian faith cannot be expressed immediately and unambiguously by a certain type of morality. The idea of a Christian ethic as such only reflects the dream of a Christian system.

Faced with this progressive loss of objective identification references Christian identity is in crisis. The signs of this crisis are numerous throughout modern times. As the attempt to root identity unambiguously in objective references such as church membership, doctrine or moral behaviour is shown to be more and more impossible, the task of identification becomes more subjective. It goes through mediations which must be accepted individually. To illustrate this aspect, we will look for a moment at an example from the nineteenth century recalling some features of the thought of Kierkegaard.

(c) Identity, the individual's existential search

In the context of our reflections, it is interesting to note that Kierkegaard's criticism, with his specific point of view, is directed particularly at the three areas of objective identification that we have just mentioned.

(i) He argues against the Danish Christian State and particularly against the equivalence which it sees between national identity, church membership and Christian identity. Christianity is held up to ridicule in a situation where one is Christian because one is Danish—this is to say, by birth. This is why Kierkegaard seeks to reintroduce Christianity into the Christian State.

(ii) In his criticism of German idealism, particularly that of Hegel, Kierkegaard underlines the error which lies in making the Christian faith an object of knowledge, even of absolute knowledge. In the matter of faith, it is not a question of intellectual adherence, but of existential acquisition. For this reason, Kierkegaard is anxious to distinguish carefully in Christianity between doctrine and the existential message.

(iii) In the same way, Kierkegaard rejects the moralisation of the Christian faith. In fact, by placing the religious in the realm of the existential, he emphasises that the link with the ethical dimension must be effected from this angle. In this way, existential passion transcends ethical tasks; it can sometimes even lead to a suspension of ethics,[2] but in all cases to their reorientation.

Thus, as we see, for this nineteenth century author, the traditional references of identification have become problematic. They must be transcended, and Kierkegaard effects this by deliberately turning towards subjectivity. Identity is a matter of existential acquisition, and the Christian is Christian in the way he is, the way he leads his life, understanding it and fulfilling it in truth. It is in this sense that one must understand Kierkegaard's thesis according to which 'truth is subjectivity'.[3] Truth and non-truth or, to use our terms, the identity and the alienation of a man, are decided not by his attachments, his knowledge and his behaviour, but by his way of living truthfully amid the constant tensions of his existence. This task, because it is subjective, is that of the individual, and that is why Kierkegaard will say that the category of the individual is the decisive category.[4] It is the individual who, as a responsible person, answers for his truth and his identity. He is singled out, called to the task of acquisition. 'In the spiritual field, a man's thoughts must be the house in which he lives—if not, too bad for them.'[5]

The concepts used by Kierkegaard have often caused misunderstandings, particularly when they have been interpreted in the light of existentialist philosophies which claim to be inspired by them. It is necessary, therefore, to reconsider these notions freely, transferring them slightly into the problem area of identity.

2. THE PROBLEM OF IDENTITY AS A SPIRITUAL TASK

In a description of the search for identity, if one seeks to avoid the usual failings, the following points should be clearly noted.

(i) The category of the individual might well suggest the idea of a personal withdrawal into self. Yet this category is fundamentally relational and interactional. Man is an individual not in some sort of ivory tower, but in the very midst of the multiple relationships which characterise his life. He is therefore placed at the busy crossroads of a multiplicity of aspects which react with each other or, to use the systematic term, which 'construct a system': the psychological, the biological, the social, the political, the ethical, the religious, etc.

(ii) At this crossroads, the identity which allows man to know himself at one with himself cannot be a static fact which closes him in upon himself; it is a dynamic process of constant integration of different aspects. It is thus constituted as a system of convictions aiming to give man a global understanding of himself, which will allow him precisely to open himself to everything which is offered to him.

(iii) Such an identity, to take Erikson's words, 'is never "fixed", never "complete" '. As a dynamic process, it is only given to man in partial and precarious syntheses in which he feels in harmony with himself without ever being able to halt the movement of his life which risks taking him far away from himself again.

(iv) In his psychogenetic analysis of identity, Erikson lays stress throughout all the stages of human life on the importance of the different identity *crises* which punctuate evolution. In a parallel way, we can also say that an identity which is only given in partial syntheses introduces the dimension of crisis into life. These crises remind man that his identity is not fixed once and for all and therefore freely at his disposal, but must be constantly recast through the shocks and questionings of existence. As Erikson emphasises, the concept of crisis can be taken here in a positive sense, 'not to describe the threat of a catastrophe, but a turning point, a crucial period of increased vulnerability and accentuated potentiality and, hence, the source (...) of creative force but also of instability'.[6]

(v) Conceived in this way as a dynamic process, identity becomes very profoundly linked to the development of man's personal life history, a life history subject to many ups and downs. Identity is not a substratum, an abstract quintessence situated beyond tensions and crises. On the contrary, as a constant process of identification, it is constituted as concrete identity *within* the fabric of the adventures and varied fortunes of personal life history. To quote the words of Ricoeur, one might say that it is in a sense the 'plot' of this history and is therefore given a sort of 'narrative identity',[7] an identity in which man can, within the unity of a story, describe himself in the events, the experiences, the tragedies, the joys and the sorrows of his life.

(vi) Taken in this context, the search for identity becomes a task which inspires the whole life of man. One can even say that as such, it makes this life a truly spiritual one because it is dynamic and open.

What we have just briefly described in general terms in the six preceding points is also valid from the Christian point of view. The Christian declaration addresses itself to man in his search for identity. It seeks to suggest to him a possible identification which allows him to place himself truthfully within the multiple aspects of his experience of life. The aim of this offer is not to 'complete' the search but rather to make of it the plot of the adventures and vicissitudes of a believing existence. This Christian identity, described here, narratively speaking, as the plot of a believing existence through its tensions, crises, joys and vicissitudes, is offered to man through a word which comes from outside himself to call upon his innermost self, which therefore comes to set him apart from himself to allow him to discover himself.

3. THE DANGER OF SUBJECTIVISM AND THE CRITICAL FUNCTION OF OBJECTIVITY

Our thoughts so far have led us to discover the danger of the objectivisation of identity. In fact, when what we have called the objective references of identification become the determining principle, identity tends to become fixed, crystallising itself on the characteristics which are judged to be representative of what everyone's identity should be. By placing this tendency for objectivisation in crisis, modern evolution makes us rediscover the truly spiritual dimension of the subjective search for identity. This is what we have tried to underline, inspired by Kierkegaard.

And yet, following this line of argument do we not run the risk of ending up at the opposite danger of subjectivism pure and simple? Is there still a place for a real exchange and debate, or must we accept the notion that 'everyone has his own truth'? What part can objectivity have here?

To answer these questions we will draw inspiration from the hypotheses formulated by P. Paroz. In his work *Faith and Reason*, devoted to a dialogue with the critical rationalism of Hans Albert, Paroz, starting from Kierkegaard, tries to show how one can avoid the shortcomings of subjectivism by articulating subjective and objective truth and instituting, from the point of view of truth, a critical inspection of the subjective by the objective.[8] It seems possible to apply this epistemological idea to our theme of identity.

(a) Subjectivism as 'immunisation' of identity

In our description of the subjective search for identity, we have placed much stress on the aspect of an open and dynamic process. Subjectivism reverses the view: identity closes itself to the challenges of the outside and withdrawing into itself, becomes fixed. In fact, by setting up paradoxically the relativist idea that 'everyone has his own truth' as a general principle, valid for all, subjectivism effectively kills all confrontation, all real exchange and debate. Subjectivity no longer has to answer for itself because it is no longer called to account. It preserves itself by eliminating all possibility of calling it in question. With critical rationalism, Paroz calls this subjectivist attitude an 'immunisation' against any critical evaluation. In contrast to such an 'immunisation' it should be emphasised that true subjectivity is not subjectivist, and that the search for identity could not be carried out on a subjectivist basis. We must outline what that means from the point of view of the relationship between subjectivity and objectivity.

(b) Subjectivity put to the test by objectivity

Subjectivism sets out to close up subjectivity within itself, cutting off all connection with the outside. Now, it must be clearly emphasised that subjectivity is essentially relational: it lies within the fabric of the complex and harsh realities of the human condition. This anchorage constitutes for it a challenge which calls it to account. If it develops an identity, a system of convictions which allows it to be in harmony with itself, it will have to answer for this identity in its own reality. In other words: its identity will be put to the test by the things of life with which it is confronted. The effort to lead a life in truth and harmony with oneself has to be made in concrete terms, in the light and the responsible acceptance of the experiences, the tasks and the examinations which make up the material of human reality. We may note that, contrary to the arbitrary nature of subjectivism, this test allows a critical examination and therefore an evaluation of identities and an authentic debate between them, the main concern of which becomes the question of their respective relevance and of their respective capacity truthfully to clarify and accept the human condition.

(c) Christian identity put to the test

The Christian faith might be tempted to exclude itself immediately from this debate, declaring itself alone capable of giving man his only true identity. Such a procedure would be tantamount to a sort of 'Christian subjectivism' or, more generally 'revelationary positivism'. From our point of view, we must reject this religious immunisation and accept the requirement of a test of Christian identity. The system of convictions of the believer must face the task of answering for its way of clarifying and accepting the stuff of human reality and, in this way, enter openly into the debate on identities without right away claiming an exclusive right to relevance. So we can talk here of an 'objective examination' of Christian identity. This examination can take many different forms. To illustrate it, we would like to return to the three aspects mentioned above—cf. 1(*b*), 1(*c*)—to make quite clear the danger of objectivisation. In fact, taken in the perspective of a critical function of objectivity, these three dimensions can become as many useful tests for Christian identity.

(i) *The interplay of relationships, or the test of how others see one.* We have seen that the interplay of the many social relationships in life plays an important role in the establishment of identity. The subjectivist attitude consists of neutralising these interactions. The Christian, mindful of his subjective search, on the other hand, even if he does not draw his identity from his relationships is certainly not going to reject them. On the contrary, he will accept them, forcing himself to live them in the light of his convictions. His different attachments, ecclesiastical, social, economic, political, will thus become an area of constant test. In fact they are for him the area of the *experience of intersubjectivity*, to which he will expose himself without reserve. In his relations with others, he meets other human beings who also live according to systems of convictions, identical or different. This intersubjective dimension of meeting with others is a component part of the search for identity. As Erikson so well expresses it: '(...) the formation of identity calls into play a process (...) by which the individual judges himself in the light of what he discovers to be the way in which others judge him in comparison with themselves and through a typology, significant in their eyes; at the same time, he judges their way of judging him in the light of his personal perception of himself, in comparison with them and with the types whom he sees as prestigious.'[9] By opening himself to dialogue with others, in the Church and more widely among his fellow men, the Christian exposes his Christian identity to the test of how others see him, a challenge which takes him to task, because it can shake his faith and plunge him into crisis.

(ii) *Doctrinal clarification, or the examination of intelligible language.* The subjective Christian does not draw his identity from the intellectual adherence to a doctrine. Yet it is none the less true that the discipline of doctrinal reflection constitutes an important task for him. In fact, the immunisation tactic of the subjectivist will push him to hide the arbitrary nature of his convictions in wooliness and vagueness. On the other hand, from the viewpoint of a truly spiritual search for identity, it is crucial to expose oneself to critical inspection by explaining one's convictions *in clear and intelligible language*. If the believer accepts in this way to account for his convictions by expressly *declaring* them, he exposes them to intelligent examination. By the objective means of articulate language, he questions himself and lets himself be questioned about the strength, the coherence and the relevance of his faith. That constitutes a real spiritual challenge, a dialogue between faith and reason, which should be neither conciliatory nor aggressive, but which can be calm and serene without lacking anything in ardour or passion.

(iii) *The ethical task, or the trial of practical relevance.* We have already said that to associate Christian identity at once with a certain type of behaviour amounts to an improper objectivisation. It will therefore never be possible to end up with an unambiguous expression of faith in the fulfilment of ethical tasks, an expression which would be like an ethical check of Christian identity.[10] Yet the ethical task, if it is not the grounds for a check, is the grounds for a test which continually causes the trial of the *practical relevance* of identity which the Christian faith claims to confer. This is what is underlined in the first epistle of John when he says: 'If a man says, "I love God", while hating his brother, he is a liar.' (4:20) Thus, committing himself to the round of practical tasks, the subjective Christian exposes his convictions to this decisive test: do they allow me to place myself convincingly in the world and to open myself to the demands which are made on me? Do my convictions enslave me, or do they give me the freedom to love my neighbour as myself? In this critical examination the believer will be on the look-out—in all restraint and humility—not for reassuring confirmation, but rather for discrepancies and faults which will be for him the crises within which his identity can grow and mature.

4. BY WAY OF CONCLUSION: CONFIDENCE IN CRISES

Whoever says critical examination or test says crisis, as we have just seen, and whoever says crisis, says judgment.[11] Thus, the subjective identity which allows itself to be tested by objective fields is an identity which, prepared to run the risk of identity crises, exposes itself deliberately to the judgment which these crises bring. The question which arises here is: is this the price of authentic identity? Is the insecurity implied by this exposure to judgment not too great? Or, to put the question differently: what is it that permits identity to expose itself in this way to the judgment of crises? For Erikson, the fundamental fact which will determine the whole progress of development is the *basic confidence* or the *basic suspicion* which the individual acquires from the first stage of his search for identity.[12] It is at this stage that the ability to open oneself or not to later crises is determined.

Transferred into our more existential perspective, the question would be: where does this confidence come from which allows man not to close himself, but to open himself to the crises which inspire his ceaseless search for identity through the vicissitudes of life? The Christian reply to this question is clear. Expressed in narrative terms, Christian identity is the adventure of a meeting with Jesus Christ, of a life shared with Him on the path which leads Him to the Cross. Such an adventure, by its unexpected and overwhelming nature, takes us out of ourselves, sets us apart from ourselves and therefore places us in a situation of crisis. The identity in which we rediscover ourselves is given in the very heart of this crisis in which we lose ourselves. 'He who loses his life will save it.' Or, to express it in the terms of the theology of the Cross: in the judgment, in the crisis of the Cross the grace of God is expressed, and this grace is sufficient to place confidence in God in crises, accepting them as so many blessed opportunities to grow in Christian identity. That is what allows one to expose oneself without equivocation to the test of how others see one, to the examination of doctrinal clarification and to the trial of practical relevance.

Translated by Barrie Mackay

Notes

1. E. H. Erikson *Adolescence et crise. La quête de l'identité* (Paris 1972) (*Identity. Youth and Crisis* (1968)) p. 20. The following reflections are inspired, without always indicating so explicitly, by the works of Erikson.

2. Cf. on this subject the treatment of the figure of Abraham in *Crainte et tremblement* (1843), in *Oeuvres complètes* (Paris 1972) vol. 5, pp. 97–209.

3. Cf. on this point the *Post-scriptum définitif et non-scientifique aux Miettes philosophiques* (1846), in *Oeuvres complètes* (Paris 1977) vols. 10 and 11, especially vol. 10, pp. 176–232. It is in this work that Kierkegaard articulates objectivity and subjectivity most clearly.

4. On this subject, cf. P. Bühler 'L'Individu. Quelques réflexions à propos d'une catégorie oubliée', *Revue d'Histoire et de Philosophie Religieuse 58* (1978) pp. 193–215.

5. S. Kierkegaard *Journal(extraits)* (Paris, vol. 1: 1834–1846, 1963) p. 392 (*Papirer*, VII A 82).

6. *Op. cit.* (cf. note 1) p. 98.

7. Cf. the recent work of Paul Ricoeur on narration. On 'narrative identity', cf. in particular an article with this title ('l' identité narrative') which will shortly appear in P. Bühler/J.-F. Habermacher (eds.) *La narration. Quand le récit devient communication* (Geneva).

8. P. Paroz *Foi et raison. La foi chrétienne aux prises avec le rationalisme critique: Hans Albert et G. Ebeling* (Geneva 1985) especially pp. 103–153 (for the theoretical model).

9. *Op. cit.* (cf. note 1) pp. 18–19.

10. Against the Calvinist idea of the third use of the Law as it is presented in E. Fuchs *La Morale selon Calvin* (Paris 1986) p. 55: 'Par son obéissance à la Loi, le croyant vérifie en quelque sorte la vérité de la foi.'

11. This is the meaning of the Greek *krisis*.

12. Cf. *op. cit.* pp. 99–110 and 97 (synthetic table).

PART II

In the View of Others

François Chavannes

An Unbeliever's View of Christian Identity

AT FIRST it may seem rather paradoxical, so many years after his death, to cite Camus' image of Christianity in order to help the reader grasp an unbeliever's notion of Christian identity. After all, Camus died some thirty years ago, and in those three decades Christianity has moved on. The external aspect presented to non-Christians has changed too. Therefore Camus' image of Christian behaviour is somewhat outdated. For instance, he maintained more than once that Christian faith led to an acceptance of injustice and to submissiveness in the face of evil. It would be difficult nowadays to hold such a view without making certain reservations. In recent years, in several countries, Christianity has become a force which questions and even counters injustice.

Nevertheless, even if Camus' understanding of Christianity now seems rather anachronistic, much of it is still relevant. Camus never tried to express the reality of human life, as he saw it, in a cohesive system of thought. His main aim was to be human and to capture his own human experience in his writings, without glossing over changes and contradictions. He wrote in 1952: 'I am not a philosopher, I can speak only of what I have actually experienced'.[1] He was able to express in forceful yet appealing prose sentiments and problems which many of his contemporaries perceived in less refined ways. That is the secret of his influence and of the present relevance of what he wrote.

Camus stood outside Christianity and described it as he saw it, from without. That image, which now seems very negative, is derived mainly from his early works. In the last few years of his life he would seem to have held a more favourable view of the Christian religion. But such a development is scarcely apparent in his works. We know of it from the testimony of some of his friends. Like many non-believers, Camus distinguished Christ as an individual and his message from Christianity as it had developed in history, which he assessed harshly.

In this article I shall try to describe the image of Christianity offered in Camus' works and to emphasise its negative aspects: those which were unacceptable to Camus and to many others who are now outside Christianity. His understanding of Christianity may be defined on the basis of the following propositions:

1. A desire for happiness and a passion for living are the essential human impulses.
2. Christianity, however, misconstrues and denies these essential urges.
3. Moreover it deprives human life of its real weight.

I shall discuss these points in the above order.

1. DESIRE FOR HAPPINESS AND PASSION FOR LIVING

Albert Camus was born in 1913. His father was a farm labourer who died on the Marne in 1914. His mother was illiterate, and to keep her children had to go out charring in the Belfort district of Algiers where she lived. Though Camus experienced poverty in childhood and youth he was not unhappy. He told René Char: 'Life was hard for us but I was very happy most of the time'.[2] These happy times included, for instance, those summer evenings when they put chairs in front of the house to enjoy the fresh air: 'His little chair was cracked, and gave way somewhat under him. But he raised his eyes to drink in the pure night ... The stars twinkled in the mysterious summer nights above'.[3]

Camus was alive to the common human pleasures of childhood and youth. He adored his affectionate yet reticent mother. He loved sun and sea, as he did the football team he belonged to from his fifteenth to seventeenth years of age. In 'Return to Tipasa' he recalls how he felt on charabanc trips to some of the beaches near Algiers: 'A vibrant childhood, adolescent daydreams against the drone of the motor-coach, mornings, fresh young girls, beaches, continually taut young muscles, slight evening tension in a sixteen-year-old heart, and ever and again the same sky over the years, with its perennial power and light'.[4]

In *Weddings* Camus allows his lust for life full rein. He gives a lyrical description of the locality of Tipasa and the happiness he experiences as he approaches the hills by the sea. He is not looking for solitude. On the contrary, he says: 'I often went there with people I liked'.[5] In such surroundings all one's senses are aroused. A kind of intoxication induces oblivion of everything other than direct sensation. This kind of overflowing is a call to love with abandon. The union of bodies is seen as a natural partaking of happiness which 'achieves equilibrium in space'. 'Here I understand what is known as glory: the right to love without restraint. There is only one love in this world. To embrace a woman's body also means grasping that odd pleasure which comes down from the sky to the sea'. Camus attacks those whose fear of pleasure would deprive him of his own. He acknowledges that he is contented and proud to have known 'the joyful relaxation of a marriage with the world'.

The happiness of Tipasa is no mere sensual indulgence.[6] It goes with a kind of universal ecstasy. The harmony of sky and sea, the richness of life which surrounds the stone pillars, are able to arouse wonder in anyone who becomes aware of them. They demonstrate a concord or relationship of humanity with the world. They elicit a love which goes beyond the sensual. 'No, it was not I who was important, nor the world, but only the concord and the silence which produced love between it and me'. Camus believed sometimes that he had sensed the underlying meaning of existence, and it was in places like Tipasa that he experienced this feeling. When, on several occasions, he said that he felt the presence of the sacred, he was referring to such moments.

Camus also experienced unhappiness: the pain of an absent father, and the material and cultural impoverishment of his family. When he was seventeen tuberculosis made him give up football and later on prevented him from going through with his teacher's examination. He married when he was twenty and ended the union two years later. When asked about this, he said that it was a 'painful experience'.[7] Afterwards he lived through the hard struggles of the Resistance, and the courageous standpoints which brought him contempt and loneliness. Nevertheless, in 1951 he acknowledged in an interview that 'when I try to decide what is essential in me, I end up with the longing for happiness. I have a very vital liking for individuals ... There is an unquenchable sun at the centre of my work.[8]

2. CHRISTIANITY MISCONSTRUES AND DENIES THESE ESSENTIAL URGES

In his lecture to the Latour-Maubourg Dominicans in Paris in 1946, Camus said: 'Since I do not feel that I have any absolute truth or any message, I shall never abandon the principle that Christian truth is an illusion, but only inasmuch as I have found it impossible to enter'.[9] Camus stayed outside Christianity not mainly for intellectual but for existential and life reasons. He felt rebuffed by Christianity since it did not recognize the value of certain human experiences which he had undergone and which provided his life with savour and meaning. Ingrid Di Meglio confirms this when she says of Camus: 'The young author expresses from his very first works onwards his belief that his own life-experience is incompatible with Christian faith'.[10] This incompatibility was mainly the result of a Christian instruction which endowed God with a countenance that aroused fear and that gave human beings a humiliated aspect.

(a) A God who is feared and worshipped, not one who laughs with human beings

In a letter of 1951 to Jean Grenier, Camus acknowledges that there is a gap between the religious feeling which he experiences naturally and that expressed in Christianity. He admits this in the form of a question: 'What am I to admire and love here [in Christianity] when I have felt that I had a religious soul only before sea or night?'[11] Any sense of the divine which Camus experienced, as recorded in the last paragraph, was felt before the beauty of nature and the universe. He found it when contemplating at night a mysterious sky with twinkling stars, or when he discovered in certain Mediterranean landscapes the unusual relationship which bound him to the world and enabled him to be himself and to fulfil himself. Yet the Christian God revealed himself to Camus in very different guises. After visiting a baroque church in Prague Camus described his impressions thus: 'The god worshipped there was the one feared and honoured, not the one who laughs with humankind before the fierce play of sea and sun'.[12] That was the same god whom he recalled in 'Weddings at Tipasa', and found himself able to acknowledge, even though there was no place for such a deity in Christianity as Camus knew it.

(b) The image of mankind humiliated

In his first works, up to *The Fall*, which appeared in 1956, Camus strongly asserted human innocence. At the same time he attacked Christian pessimism: that is, a form of Christian instruction which assigned guilt and made sin predominant, to the disadvantage of human nature and made it impossible for humans to do good without the aid of grace. In spring 1942 he recorded the following in his *Notebooks*: 'We help a person more by giving him a favourable image of himself than by constantly confronting him with his faults ... For two thousand years man has been offered a humiliated image of himself. The result is obvious'.[13] Once again, in December 1946, during his lecture to the Latour-Maubourg Dominicans, Camus directly attacked this humiliated image of mankind which he thought Christianity used in its teaching. Accordingly he said: 'It was not I who invented the wretchedness of human beings or the awful edicts of the divine curse. I did not utter this "Nemo Bonus" or the damnation of unbaptised children. I did not say that man could not obtain his own salvation and that from the depths of his degradation his only hope was in divine grace ... Christianity is pessimistic in regard to man, but optimistic in respect of human destiny. I however am pessimistic in regard to human destiny and optimistic in respect of man'.[14]

In somewhat different terms, many unbelievers today would align themselves with Camus here. They are pessimistic in regard to human destiny because they do not believe in resurrection. They are optimistic in respect of man, who they think is good rather than evil. They reject the idea of sin and the feeling of guilt which, they say, is linked to it. Surely the indifference of the young is partly connected with the fact that in their eyes the Church subdues life and the verve of life? Instead of being heard as a summons to live, surely the gospel message has been received as a collection of prohibitions? A confirmand who was asked how he saw religion answered: 'Religion is what must not be done'.[15] It is significant, too, that a child drew a priest when asked to picture the man of sorrows.

When it stresses the fear of God and human guilt, Christianity counters the desire for happiness and the passion for life which are in human beings. Moreover, according to Camus, Christian faith would result in a devaluation of life in this world.

3. CHRISTIANITY DEPRIVES LIFE OF ITS REAL STRENGTH

On three occasions we find in Camus' writing this idea that religious faith 'releases man from the burden of his own life'.[16] In its context, this expression means that hope in a life beyond death devalues life in the here and now, just as acceptance of a universally explanatory doctrine unburdens man of the weight of his freedom.

(a) Hope in a life beyond death devalues life in the here and now

In *Weddings* Camus describes how he felt when he came upon the ruins of Djemila. The bare location gave him a sense of his own destitution and the 'taste of death' which he shared with this dead city. This feeling of death made him write: 'I obstinately reject all the "laters" of this world because it is just as important not to give up its present riches. I do not like to think that death is the door to another life. For me it is a closed door. I do not say that it is a step which has to be taken but that it is a vile and dirty experience.

Everything which is suggested to me amounts to depriving man of the burden of his own life'.[17]

Camus rejects all the 'laters' of this world, primarily because he does not wish to be relieved of the burden of his own death. His death is relativised, even elided by hope in another life. A Dominican was crude enough to say in Camus' presence 'that death was only of very relative importance in human destiny'. Father Bruckberger, who describes the occurrence, adds: 'Camus never forgot this. He mentioned it to me years later'.[18] There is a careless way of speaking about death and resurrection which cancels their mystery and suppresses the serious and tragic aspect of life.

Even though Camus rejects all the 'laters' in the world, the main reason is because he does not want to reject its 'present riches'. He senses that hope in eternity could involve devaluing life. This risk is genuine. The lives of the martyrs show that a considerable number of them were quite indifferent to earthly reality: compared with the glory that awaited them, it seemed contemptible. Similarly, some mystics who have experienced divine union have felt acutely the vanity of worldly reality. Finally, hope in eternal life offers the certainty of an ultimate victory of good over evil, but runs the risk of devaluing the struggle for greater justice. Why struggle if victory is assured? 'Christianity in history', Camus writes, 'relegates to a point beyond history the cure of evil and of the slaughter which are nevertheless endured in history ... For twenty centuries, the sum total of evil has not diminished in the world'.[19]

On the contrary, according to Camus, acceptance of a death without hope endows life in the here and now with value. Mere everyday reality, the discovery of beauty, the meeting of individuals, struggle for justice, take on a value which cannot be simulated. The ephemeral nature of these realities, far from devaluing them, enables us to love and admire them more. Hence Camus found 'excellent' Newman's remark that we should admire the things of this world at the moment in which we surrender them'.[20] And we renounce them in a definitive way at the moment of our death. Speaking of human relations and of friendship between people, Camus notes that 'These are the true riches because they are perishable'.[21] Finally, he recalls the tenor of his first works when he writes: 'If there is a sin against life, it is probably not so much in despairing of it as in hoping for another life, and avoiding the unrelenting splendour of this one'.[22]

(b) Christianity deprives man of the burden of his freedom

In *The Myth of Sisyphus* Camus explains as follows what seems to be the basic obstacle keeping him outside Christianity: 'Then I understand why the universally explanatory doctrines also diminish me. They deprive me of the burden of my own life yet I still have to bear it alone'.[23] To be deprived of the burden of one's own life means, at present, accepting a doctrine which, while explaining everything, tells people how to behave. Such an acceptance deprives people of what is most precious: their moral freedom and independence.

Yet such, according to Camus, is the condition of the believer. He must obey God, yet that obedience takes the form of submission to the teaching of the churches: 'It is a doctrine which they provide and one has to adhere to it'.[24] By accepting this doctrine uncritically, the believer surrenders his own individual thinking and guidance. Thus he loses his freedom. Camus cannot accept such a renunciation. He wants a full assumption of his own life and thought: 'A deep thought is a continual process of becoming, it encounters a life experience and moulds itself upon it'.[25] For Camus, progress towards enlightened truth, in the sense of a practical truth about how one ought to behave in life, takes the form of a permanent confrontation of already acquired beliefs with new facts which contradict them. It also occurs in dialogue with other people. But nothing is so contrary to this progress towards truth than the argument of an authority which suppresses all debate and all inquiry. Talking to students after the Budapest uprising of 1956, Camus said: 'Remember what we have just experienced in order to remain loyal to freedom, both to its rights and to its duties, and in order never to accept that anyone, however important he may be, or any party, however strong it may be, should think for you and tell you how to behave'.[26] A man worthy of the name can never accept that a party or church should think in his stead and force on him the behaviour that he should manifest himself.

This submission of believers to an official doctrine releases a sickness which is more especially experienced by those in positions of authority in the Church. Camus reveals this sickness in the conduct which he assigns to Father Paneloux, a character in *The Plague*. At the beginning of the novel, Father Paneloux lives 'abstractedly'[27] because he identifies with the official message of the Church. It is this message, as he conceives it, which he preaches in his first sermon: the plague is a punishment, we must submit to it because God desires it. Shortly afterwards, Paneloux is present while a child dies very painfully. He emerges from 'abstraction' and gives a very different sermon. He no longer tries to pronounce the official message of the Church, but says what he really thinks: that is, that we do not understand the child's suffering; it is a scandal for the soul and for the heart.

Paneloux uses two different but successive voices. A serious phenomenon today is that believers, priests especially, find it necessary to speak two languages. Since they cannot in conscience accept certain official viewpoints of the Church (in the domain of sexual morality for example) they express themselves differently in public and private. In public they cannot diverge from official teaching, whereas in private they talk freely and say what they really think. This sickness, so painfully experienced inside the Church, is also perceived by non-believers who are scandalised by the hypocrisy of such behaviour.

4. CONCLUSION

By the end of this analysis, it would seem that the image of Christianity found in the writings of Albert Camus is very negative. There Christian life is described as anti-life and Christian behaviour as anti-human behaviour. It is true that the writer is separate from the work, but it is the work which is read, whereas the development of Camus' personal thought largely escapes us. This negative understanding of Christianity poses numerous serious questions for the Christian conscience. I shall mention three in conclusion.

Non-believers like Camus have experiences which seem to them incompatible with Christian faith. They have a lively taste for happiness, for example, admire everything which is beautiful, demand justice and in short have a passion for living whose strength seems to them to be denied by Christianity as they discern it. Jean Grenier reports the following words of Camus': 'Father X is a believer not out of weakness but out of fulness of life. Usually it is out of weakness'.[28] Can one be a Christian out of fulness of life? That is the first question asked of Christianity by Camus' understanding of it.

The second question concerns the devaluation of life in the present. It may be put thus: Is it possible to live in communion with the Absolute without the value of the relative being destroyed? Christian faith, by asking us to enter into communion with God now and for eternity, surely causes us to value wrongly this world and certain human realities which make it up. By making us see this world *sub specie aeternitatis*, that is, in its relation to God and to eternity, surely faith leads us to empty this world of its due substance, and to hold cheap that in it which is only perishable in order to value only that part of it which remains for ever'?

The third question has to do, once again, with reference to the absolute, but this time in the teaching of the Church. Inasmuch as this teaching is presented as an explanation of the Word of God, it acquires an absolute authority. The believer has to submit to it. Yet, while exercising its authority, the Church has surely on occasion committed the 'sombre error' of which Camus speaks, which consists in 'assigning to God what is not God's'.[29] In particular, it seems to decide for believers what they are to think, and how they should act in areas which do not directly derive from faith, thus removing from them a free space to which they are entitled.

These are not new questions, and need not be new to remain relevant. Some people will be astonished that the problem of evil has not been touched on when it occupies a major place in Camus' works. It would seem that the main question which Camus directs at Christianity is not linked to the problem of evil but to that of the world's lack of value: reference to an Absolute, requiring, according to him, a devaluation of present-day life. It is on that point that I have centred these reflections.[30]

5. SUGGESTION

Believers, and much more obviously theologians, cannot remain indifferent to the questions posed by Camus. The author of this article thanks those who agree to let him know their thoughts on the subject. These will help him to complete 'A study in progress entitled "Christian Reflections" on the Basis of Questions posed to Christianity by the Works of Albert Camus'. Please send your comments to: François Chavannes, 92 rue Didouche Mourad, 16006 Algiers, Algeria.

Translated by J. G. Cumming

Notes

1. Letter to *Libertaire* (1952) II, p. 753. References are to the two volumes of Camus' writings in the Pléiade edition: I and II.
2. Letter of 1953, II, p. 1180.
3. 'L'Envers et L'Endroit', II, p. 24–25.
4. 'Eté', II, p. 872.
5. This and the following quotations are from 'Noces à Tipasa', II, pp. 56–60.
6. Later Camus was to acknowledge the defects of unbridled sexuality and the riches of chastity: 'There is a time when sex is a victory—when it emerges from moral imperatives. But it soon becomes a defeat—and the sole victory is won over it in its turn, and that is chastity', *Carnets* 2, p. 51.
7. Interview with C. A. Viggiani.
8. Interview with G. d'Aubarède (1951) II, p. 1339.
9. II, p. 371.
10. '*Revue des Lettres modernes*; Serie A. Camus' No. 11, p. 27.
11. *A. Camus—J. Grenier Correspondance*, p. 181.
12. 'La Mort Heureuse', p. 105.
13. *A. Camus—Carnets 2*, p. 16.
14. II, pp. 373–374. Later Camus was to recognise a human guilt. His position on this point was to come closer to the Christian viewpoint. (It was in the writings of St Augustine that Camus read of the damnation of children who had died unbaptised).
15. Heinz Zahrnt *A l'Ouest d'Eden* p. 207.

16. 'Noces', II, p. 63. 'Le Mythe de Sisyphe', I, pp. 139 and 210.
17. 'Vent a Djemilas', II, p. 63.
18. *NRF*, No. 87, pp. 517–518.
19. 'L'Homme revolté', II, p. 706.
20. *A. Camus—J. Grenier Correspondance*, p. 89.
21. 'Le Mythe de Sisyphe', II, p. 167.
22. 'Noces', II, p. 76. Nevertheless, Camus wrote in *The Plague*: 'He [Rieux] had become aware of the sterile aspects of a life without illusions. There is no peace without hope', I, p. 1459.
23. 'Le Mythe de Sisyphe', II, p. 139.
24. 'Le Mythe de Sisyphe', II, p. 167.
25. *Ibid.* II, p. 190.
26. 'Message en faveur de la Hongrie' (1956), II, p. 1782.
27. For Camus, people live in abstraction when they accept an ideology or a doctrine which screens them from reality and prevents them from seeing it as it is. In his Latour-Maubourg lecture Camus said: 'What the world expects from Christians ... is that they should emerge from abstraction and confront the bloody countenance which history has assumed in our times' (II, p. 373).
28. *Albert Camus—Souvenirs*, p. 139.
29. 'Le Mythe de Sisyphe', II, p. 207.
30. My centring of these observations on the devaluation of Christian life through its reference to the Absolute, as well as the concluding remarks, are much indebted to verbal observations by Christian Duquoc.

Masao Abe

Transformation in Buddhism in Comparison with Platonic and Christian Notions

I

TRANSFORMATION IN Buddhism centres in the realisation of death. Apart from the realisation of death the Buddhist notion of transformation cannot be legitimately grasped. This is true of the transformation of society as well as the transformation of the individual.

What, then, is the realisation of death? Dōgen, a Japanese Zen master of the thirteenth century, said, 'It is a mistake to understand that one passes from life to death'.[1] In our daily life we usually think that we are now alive but that we may die sometime in the future: we think of ourselves as gradually moving from life to death. Dōgen insisted that this ordinary understanding of life and death is a mistake. In our usual way of thinking life and death are distinguished from one another—and their relationship is taken as a *process* that moves from life to death. Here we must pose a question to ourselves. When we consider the relationship between life and death in this way—*where* are we taking our stand? In life or in death? Or do we take a stand somewhere else? When we look upon the relation of life and death as a *process* moving from the former to the latter, our 'existential' posture is *outside* of both. It is just like standing on an embankment and looking down the river of life flowing from its source to its lower reaches. Are we, not, however, actually swimming right in the middle of this river? By taking our position outside of both life and death we objectify our life as something 'present' and our death as something which will happen in the 'future'.

An objectified or conceptualised life, however, is no longer life as it is. In the same way, an objectified or conceptualised death is not actual death. An objectifying viewpoint makes no serious inquiry into the significance of life— no existential realisation of the anxiety of death. Real life cannot be viewed objectively from the outside. It must be grasped subjectively from within. For we are living our lives existentially at every moment as though we are middle of a river. Even so, one is apt to reify or substantialise both the swimming self and the flow of the river as if they were after all two different entities. This static view misses the quality of living reality. One truly grasps their own existential living only when, to use the present metaphor, the swimmer himself or herself at once seizes all together, i.e. self, swimming, and the river at one and the same time. Here the grasped and the grasper are dynamically one, not two. At this point, we come to realise fully that we are swimming in a river which, having no bottom, cannot be made into a 'thing'.

The bottomless depths of life reach down into the realm of death itself. On the other hand, the undertow of death can be felt even in the ripples of the surface. Life and death touch one another at every moment. Death is not reached only at the end of life, but is continuously present and at work throughout. Just as we can swim forward only by overcoming sinking into the bottomless depths of the river at every moment, we can live our lives only by overcoming death at each and every instant. To live our lives is no less than to continuously choose to live by rejecting the choice of death. (One can commit suicide by his or her free will.)

In the non-conceptualised, existential understanding of life and death, life and death are not two separate events, but dynamically one. Being different principles, they are opposed to one another and negate each other and yet they are inseparably connected—an existential antinomy at the depth of human existence. Or, more precisely, our being itself is nothing but this existential antinomy of life and death. Accordingly, it is not that we are moving from life to death, but that, at each and every moment, we are fully living and fully dying. Living and dying are paradoxically one. Just as the two sides of a single sheet of paper which are quite distinct and yet inseparable, 'living' and 'dying' are two different aspects of one and the same reality which are antithetical and yet inseparable. This is true throughout the spectrum of human life regardless of age. Even a new-born baby, fresh from its mother's womb, is beginning to die, or an old person on his or her death bed can be said to be living—if life and death are grasped from within existentially, not from the outside objectively.

A rigid separation of life and death is abstract and unreal. It is only a conceptual understanding of life and death, an understanding which objectifies life and death by taking its stand beyond both—in an imaginary place established by thought alone. This is the reason Dōgen said, 'It is a mistake to understand that one passes from life to death'. Accordingly, we should not speak of 'life *and* death' but 'living-dying'. One must overcome the dualistic view of life and death, and must awaken to the non-dual reality of living-dying. In truth, at each and every moment we are 'living-dying'. And yet, this living-dying process is without beginning and without end. We are continuously involved in this beginningless and endless process of living-dying. Buddhism calls this beginningless and endless process of living-dying samsara, often likening it to a great flowing ocean which is boundless and bottomless.

For Buddhists, this beginningless and endless process of living-dying in itself is regarded as 'death' in the true sense of the word. It is not death as a counterpart of life, or death in the relative sense, but death in the absolute sense. It is called 'Great Death' in Zen. Accordingly, what is problematic to Buddhists is not death as an event that counters life, but the endless process of living-dying, i.e. samsara. And thus the aim of Buddhism is not to overcome death and attain eternal life, but to be liberated from samsara, that is, the beginningless and endless process of living-dying and thereby to awaken to nirvana the blissful freedom from transmigration. Transformation in Buddhism means transformation from an existence bound by samsara to an existence liberated from samsara, i.e. existence in nirvana. For this Buddhist transformation, the realisation of the beginningless and endless process of living-dying as the true sense of absolute death is crucial. In Buddhism, transformation in the dimension of only life without the realisation of absolute death or Great Death is not true transformation. And this is the case with the transformation of society a well as with the transformation of the individual.

II

It is, however, not peculiar to Buddhism that transformation is grasped in relation to the realisation of death. If we take Plato's idea of *kathársis* to indicate a kind of transformation, we can say that in Plato's philosophy transformation is grasped through the realisation of death. To Plato, *kathársis* is purification of the soul from contamination by the body in order to prepare itself for a better life. For him, death is nothing but the purification of the soul through being released from the perished corporeal body. Death is not the body entering a tomb, but the releasing of the soul from the body (*sōma*) which is the tomb (*sēma*) of the soul (*Gorgias* 493A). Plato not only believes in the immortality of the soul after death, but also encourages philosophers to 'practice dying' while living in this world. For Plato, to philosophise means to purify (*kathársis*) the soul from bodily corruption and to contemplate the world of ideas while the soul exists within the body.

In Plato, however, the immortality of the soul and philosophy as the *kathársis* of the soul, are all based on a dualistic view of body and soul. Although the realisation of death is essential for Platonic transformation, death is grasped as the separation of the soul from the body. There is no realisation of Great Death in the Buddhist sense which is the realisation of the beginningless and endless process of living-dying as the absolute death, and in which body and soul, life and death, are grasped non-dualistically.

In this respect, Christianity is much closer to Buddhism than Platonism. In Christianity, both body and soul originate in the creation of God, and the body is not the prison of the soul as in Plato, but rather a 'temple of the Holy Spirit' (1 Cor. 6:19). What is essential to distinguish in Christianity is not the soul and body, but God and the human being. And, in Christianity, the human being must die not because of the perishability of the human body, but because of original sin. Death is grasped in Christianity not as natural death or as the separation of the imperishable soul from the perishable body, but as 'the wages of sin'. (Rom. 6:23) Through faith in the resurrection of Jesus Christ, however, Christians can look forward to eternal life in the kingdom of God beyond sin and death. Paul says of baptism as a symbol of transformation:

> When we were baptized in Christ Jesus we were baptized in his death—we went into the tomb with him and joined him in death, so that as Christ was raised from the dead—we too might live a new life. (Rom. 6:3–7)

Paul also says:

> Whereof we faint not: but though our outward man is decaying, yet our inward man is renewed day by day. (2 Cor. 4–16)

In faith in Jesus as Christ, Christians die together with Christ day by day and revive together with Christ day by day. Everyday, therefore, indeed, today, here and now, Christians die as the old person and resurrect as the new person with Christ Jesus. Thus, Christian transformation from the outward person to the inward person, from the old person to the new person is realised through one's death and resurrection together with Christ. Apart from our death and resurrection day by day, together with Christ's death and resurrection, there can be no transformation in the Christian sense. This is strikingly similar to the Buddhist understanding of transformation.

Yet, we should not overlook an essential difference between Christianity and Buddhism in the understanding of death and transformation. Unlike Plato's philosophy which regards body and soul dualistically, Christianity grasps body and soul as a unity, both in life and death. In Christianity, the body, *sarx* or *sōma*, and the soul, *pneúma* or *psyche*, though somewhat antagonistic, are equally divine creations and are always to be grasped in relation to God. God, and a person as a unity of body and soul, are related not only vitally in terms of creation, but also personally in terms of an I-Thou relationship through the Word. Death is nothing other than 'the wages of sin' as the result of rebelling against the Word of God. Transformation from the old person to the new person is only possible through faith in the death and resurrection of Jesus as Christ, the only incarnation of the Word of God in history. In short, the unity of body and soul, life, death, and resurrection, transformation from the old to the new person—all are grasped in relation to God as the Lord. In Buddhism, however, this human relationship to one God is absent—at least in the fundamental form of Buddhism (historical and doctrinal). Instead of one God as the creator, judge, and redeemer, Buddhism puts forth the principle of *pratitya-samutpada*, i.e., dependent origination, and an accompanying notion of the non-substantiality of everything in the universe. According to this Buddhist principle, everything co-arises and co-ceases with everything else; nothing exists independently. This is the reason Gautama Buddha did not accept the age-old traditional notion of Brahman as the supreme creative principle of the universe. The notion of one God as the Lord of the universe is not found in early Buddhism.

The Buddhist principle of dependent origination is inseparably connected with the rejection of dualism and monism or monotheism. From the Buddhist point of view, dualism as a theory consisting of two basic and irreducible principles cannot be true, because dualism presupposed two entities, such as body and soul as the basic principles, by objectifying and conceptualising them from the outside. Again, for Buddhism, both monism—the doctrine of one ultimate substance or principle, and monotheism—the doctrine or belief that there is but one God, cannot be true because in monism and monotheism there must be a veiled person—other than one principle or one God—who speaks of the existence of that one principle of that one God. The non-objectifiable, non-conceptual understanding of reality entails the principle of dependent origination which is neither dualistic or monistic.

Buddhism denies the notion of the soul as having an independent existence, and insists upon the non-duality of the 'body' and the 'soul' on the basis of dependent origination. And, on the same basis, as mentioned earlier, in Buddhism, life and death are grasped inseparably from one another in terms of living-dying which is without beginning and without end. In other words, Buddhism views human beings not as mortal in Plato's sense, nor as having to die because of original sin as in Christianity, but as engaged in a living-dying existence in terms of *karma*, a concept soon to be discussed.

III

In the preceding I have discussed the notion that transformation in both Christianity and Buddhism are inseparably connected with the realisation of death, but that the realisation of death in these two religions are also significantly different. In Christianity, death is grasped as the 'wages of sin', i.e. as the result of sin committed by Adam rebelling against the Word of God. On the other hand, in Buddhism, death, or living-dying is realised as karma committed by oneself from the far distant past. Just as the Christian transformation cannot be properly understood apart from the realisation of sin, the Buddhist transformation cannot be adequately grasped apart from the recognition of karma.

Why is living-dying realised as karma? And what is the religious significance of karma—an understanding of which is essential for Buddhist transformation? In order to answer these questions the following four points must be clarified.

First, as I mentioned earlier, we usually think of life and death as two different entities by objectifying or conceptualising them. In taking a dualistic view of life and death, we cling to life as a desirable state and dread death as an undesirable state. Thus, we are inevitably shackled by the opposition and conflict between life and death, not only conceptually, but also emotionally and volitionally, that is, with our whole existence. In this way we are bound over to the endless process of a life-death conflict which is called samsara in Buddhism. Accordingly, samsara does *not* mean that living-dying is *transmigration in a biological sense*, but *transmigration deeply rooted in human volition* (thirst or craving) and ignorance. As the *Samyutta-nikāya*, one of the earliest Buddhist scriptures, states:

> No beginning is known of the eternal samsara of beings, streaming and flowing to and fro [in the ocean of births and deaths], being covered by ignorance (*avijjā, avidyā*) and fettered in thirst (*tanhā*).[2]

That is why the transmigration of living-dying is understood in Buddhism as *karma* which means *act* or *deed*.[3] Our usual attachment to life and dread of death is deeply rooted in *bhāva tanhā*, the thirst or craving to be, to live, to grow more and more—an unconscious, endless impulse in human existence which Schopenhauer called the *blinder Wille zum Leben* (the blind will to live). It is also deeply rooted in *avidyā*, the fundamental ignorance of the non-duality of life and death, and of the beginninglessness and endlessness of transmigration. In Buddhism, our life and death struggle is grasped as karma because it is ultimately rooted in our *blind craving to exist*, and in our fundamental ignorance of the principle of dependent origination and the non-substantiality of everything in the universe.

Second, in order to achieve transformation in Buddhism, that is transformation from an existence involved in samsara to an existence living in nirvana, we must clearly realise: (1) the non-duality of life and death; (2) the beginninglessness and endlessness of our living-dying; and (3) the total living-dying at this moment of the absolute present.

(1) To grasp the essential of human life we must reject the dualistic view of life and death and see this as a conceptualised view lacking true reality, and must awaken to the realisation that we are living-dying at each and every moment, a realisation that comes about when we existentially grasp our life from within.

(2) We must also realise that the process of our living-dying is without beginning and without end. The process of our living-dying extends itself beyond our present life both into the direction of the remote past and into the direction of the distant future. (This is the reason, for example, Zen raises the traditional question: 'What is your original face before your parents were born'?[4] as well as the question: 'If you are free from life and death, you know where you will go. When the four elements [a physical human body] are decomposed, where do you go'?)[5] Due to the absence of God as the creator and the ruler of the universe, in Buddhism there is no beginning in terms of creation and no end in terms of last judgment. Accordingly, we must realise the beginninglessness and endlessness of samsara that is, the transmigration of living-dying. This realisation is essential because it provides a way to overcome samsara and to turn it into nirvana.

(3) The realisation of the beginninglessness and endlessness of the living-dying is inseparably linked with the realisation of our fully living-dying at each and every moment. This is because if we clearly realise the beginningless*ness* and endless*ness* of the process of living-dying *at this moment* the whole process of living-dying is concentrated *into this moment*. In other words, this moment embraces the whole process of living-dying by virtue of the clear realisation of the beginningless*ness* and endless*ness* of the process of living-dying. Here, in this point, we can overcome samsara, and realise nirvana right in the midst of samsara.

Third, the Buddhist notion of karma has *both an individual and a universal* aspect. Any karma is an act oriented by one's volition. Although it is affected by circumstances and external stimuli, fundamentally, karma is self-responsible action determined by one's will or thirst, consciously or unconsciously. Accordingly, karma is morally characterised and remains thoroughly the responsibility of each individual. At the same time, any karma affects not only the continuity of individual beings but also the solidarity of collective human existence. Due to this sympathetic or contagious character or karma, the whole universe is understood by Buddhism as the 'collective mass of karmas' of all beings.

This twofold aspect of karma, that is, the individual aspect and the universal aspect, are not exceptions to our living-dying. Rather, in Buddhism, the beginningless and endless process of our living-dying, that is, samsara, is grasped as karma deeply rooted in our blind will and ignorance and thus as karma thoroughly responsible for by each of us. And yet, at the same time, the same samsara is realised as universal karma firmly rooted in craving and fundamental ignorance which are innate in human nature. Buddhist transformation is possible only when samsara—that is, the beginningless and endless process of living-dying—is realised as karma in the above double sense, is overcome, and nirvana is realised. To be more specific, individual transformation is achieved on the basis of overcoming the individual aspect of karma, whereas the transformation of society can be realised on the basis of overcoming the universal aspect of human karma—although these two aspects are inseparably linked together.

Parenthetically speaking, the Christian notion of sin and the Buddhist notion of karma have a remarkable affinity in terms of their respective twofold aspects of *individuality and universality*. We have already seen that on the one hand, the Buddhist notion of karma is individual responsibility, and, yet, on the other hand, has a universality common to all humankind. In Christianity, the same is true of the notion of sin. As Paul says:

> Therefore, as sin came into the world through one man and death through sin, so death spread to all men because all men sinned. (Rom. 5:12)

Sin and resultant death spread to all human beings through Adam's sin. However, as Kierkegaard rightly emphasises in *The Concept of Dread*, each of us committed sin in Adam. If I am not mistaken, in Christianity, individual transformation is achieved through overcoming individual sin, whereas the transformation of society is possible on the basis of overcoming sin common to all human beings—although we should also clearly recognise the inseparability of these two aspects.

IV

Heretofore, I have tried to clarify *how* transformation takes place in Buddhism. Now, I would like to proceed to elucidate *what happens* in Buddhist transformation. In this regard, special attention will be given to the way the transformation of the individual is related to the transformation of society and to historical change.

As I mentioned earlier, Buddhist transformation is nothing but transformation from an existence living in samsara to an existence living in nirvana. This transformation is possible through overcoming karma in terms of the beginningless and endless process of living-dying. I also emphasised that this overcoming of karma is possible at each and every moment when we clearly realise the beginningless*ness* and endless*ness* of the process of living-dying and when thereby the whole process of living-dying *is concentrated into this present moment*. This means that in the midst of samsara, nirvana is fully realised.

In this connection it is important to note the following four points: First, Buddhist transformation takes place not in nirvana apart from samsara, but at the intersection of samsara and nirvana. Nirvana which is apart from samsara is not true nirvana. Nirvana is realised when the beginninglessness and endlessness of samsara is fully realised, i.e., when samsara is fully realised as samsara. A full realisation of samsara as it is, is nothing but a full realisation of nirvana. This is the reason I stated that nirvana is realised in the midst of samsara. Again, this is the reason Mahayana Buddhist scriptures emphasise that samsara is nirvana and nirvana is samsara. Accordingly, Buddhist transformation takes place not somewhere off in the distance, past or future, but right here, at this moment, right now in this actual immediate world.

Second, the statement 'samsara is nirvana, nirvana is samsara', should not be understood to signify a static or immediate identity of samsara and nirvana. In one sense, samsara is samsara; nirvana is nirvana. They are essentially different. Samsara is subjugated by karma whereas nirvana is free from karma. One must overcome attachment to samsara and arrive at nirvana. But if one stays in nirvana, stays apart from samsara, one is still selfish because abiding in nirvana one may enjoy one's own salvation while forgetting the suffering of one's fellow beings who are still involved in samsara. To be completely unselfish one should not stay in nirvana but return to the realm of samsara there to save suffering fellow beings. This is the reason Mahayana Buddhism emphasises 'In order to attain Wisdom one should not abide in samsara; in order to fulfil compassion one should not abide in nirvana'.[6] Not abiding either in samsara or nirvana, and freely moving from samsara to nirvana, from nirvana to samsara, without attaching to either, this dynamic movement is true nirvana in Mahayana Buddhism. When I stated Buddhist transformation takes place at the intersection of samsara and nirvana I referred to this dynamism of true nirvana. In Mahayana Buddhism self-awakening in nirvana, however important it may be, is not sufficient. Only when awakening others from samsara is achieved is self-awakening also achieved. Here we see the basis for the transformation of society in Buddhism.

Third, the Four Great Vows, which all Mahayana Buddhists proclaim, are as follows:

> However innumerable sentient beings are, I vow to save them;
> However inexhaustible the passions are, I vow to extinguish them;
> However immeasurable the Dharmas are, I vow to master them;
> However incomparable the Buddha-truth is, I vow to attain it.

In these 'Four Great Vows', the first vow, 'However innumerable sentient beings are, I vow to save them', is aimed at *benefiting others*, while the remaining three vows—that is, the vows to extinguish the passions, to master the Dharmas, and to attain the Buddha-truth—refer to *self-benefits*. It is worth noting that the vow for benefiting others comes before the vows for self-benefit. This signifies the spirit of the Bodhisattva, the model of the Mahayana Buddhist who strives to save others before saving oneself. One can attain true enlightenment only through helping others to attain enlightenment. Instead of becoming an enlightened being immediately, a Bodhisattva vows to save all other beings and works with compassion for the benefit of suffering beings. For the Bodhisattva, self-benefit and benefiting others are dynamically one. This is called *jiri-rita-enman*, the perfect fulfilment of self-benefit and benefiting others.

The vow of Bodhisattva to save all beings and to attain Buddhahood is a single process involving both self and others, and provides the basis for the transformation of society in Buddhism. Mahayana scriptures often talk about the construction of the Buddha Land. But, when Buddhism emphasises the perfect fulfilment of self-benefit and benefiting others, the term 'others' actually indicates other persons and not necessarily society at large. Traditional Buddhism lacks a concrete program of social transformation. This is partly because Buddhism is more concerned with the ground or religious basis for social transformation rather than a practical program, and partly because in Buddhism the ground or religious basis for social transformation is not limited to human beings but includes all beings, human and natural. It is an urgent task for Buddhism to actualise the Bodhisattva idea in a concrete plan for social transformation in the contemporary human predicament.

Fourth, in connection with the transformation of society we must pay due attention to historical change as understood in Buddhism.

Buddhism has a unique view of time. Time is understood to be entirely without beginning and without end. Since time is beginningless and endless it is not considered to be linear as in Christianity or circular as in non-Buddhist

Vedantic philosophy. Being neither linear nor circular, time is completely reversible and yet time moves from moment to moment, each moment embracing the whole process of time. Because of this unique view of time, Buddhism is relatively weak in its view of history. Time is not directly history. Time becomes 'history' when the factor of spatiality (worldhood, *Weltlichkeit*) is added to it. History comes to have meaning when time is understood to be irreversible and each moment has an unrepeatable uniqueness or the once-and-for-all nature (*Einmalichkeit*). But, since in Buddhism time is understood to be entirely beginningless and endless and thus reversible, the unidirectionality of time and the uniqueness of each moment essential to the notion of history is not clearly expressed in Buddhism.

Buddhism, however, can develop its own view of history, if we take seriously the compassionate aspect of nirvana. As I stated earlier, true nirvana in Mahayana Buddhism is not nirvana apart from samsara. Just as one must overcome attachment to samsara to attain nirvana, one must overcome attachment to nirvana to return to samsara. 'In order to attain wisdom one should not abide in samsara: in order to fulfil compassion one should not abide in nirvana' is an important admonition for Mahayana Buddhists. In the wisdom aspect of nirvana, in which samsara is done away with, everything and everyone is freed from living-dying transmigration and thereby attains its original nature. Again, in this wisdom aspect of nirvana, time ceases because the beginningless and endless process of time is totally concentrated in each moment which is realised as eternal now in the sense of *absolute present*. However, everything and everyone, though realised in its original nature in the light of wisdom, do not necessarily awaken to this basic reality. Many beings are still ignorant of this reality and are involved in the process of samsara.

Accordingly, one who has attained nirvana should not abide in nirvana but should return to the realm of samsara to help these people equally awaken to their original nature by themselves. This is the compassionate aspect of nirvana which can be actualised only by overcoming the attachment to one's own nirvana. This process of actualising the compassionate aspect of nirvana is endless because people who do not awaken to their original nature are countless and appear to be endless. Here the progress of history toward the future is necessary and comes to have a positive significance.

In the light of wisdom realised in nirvana everything and everyone awakens to their original nature and time is overcome. In the light of compassion (also realised in nirvana), however, time is religiously significant. Unidirectional history toward the future becomes essential. Here, we do have a Buddhist view of history.

It is not, however, an eschatological view of history nor a teleological view of history in the Christian or Western sense. If we use the term eschatology, the

Buddhist view of history is *a completely realised eschatology*, because in the light of wisdom everything and everyone without exception is realised in its original nature, and time is thereby overcome. If we use the term teleology, the Buddhist view of history is an *open teleology* because in the light of compassion the process of awakening others in history is endless. The completely realised eschatology and the entirely open teleology are dynamically united in this present moment, now. Buddhist transformation in history takes place dynamically at the intersection of the wisdom aspect and the compassionate aspect of nirvana.

V

With regard to the relationship between the transformation of the individual and social and historical transformation, I would now like to discuss Shin'ichi Hisamatsu's notion of FAS. Shin'ichi Hisamatsu (1889–1980) was the most outstanding Zen philosopher of mid-twentieth century Japan. He was Professor of Buddhism at Kyoto University during the period around World War II. But—far more than a scholar of Buddhism—Hisamatsu was a living personification of Zen, a man who lived his daily life and performed various activities deeply rooted in the ground of his clear-cut Zen awakening. He was an excellent tea master, calligrapher, and poet, and yet a reformer of traditional Zen in Japan.[7] All aspects of his personality and activities stemmed from a single religious realisation which he called 'awakening'.[8] His notion of FAS was not an exception to this. Rather FAS represented Hisamatsu's basic understanding of human existence on which his philosophy, religion, art, and particularly his idea of the reformation of traditional Zen, were firmly established. (Hisamatsu used this English acronym, FAS, because there is no adequate Japanese abbreviation to express his threefold notion.)

What, then, is FAS? 'F' stands for 'Awakening to the *F*ormless Self', referring to the dimension of depth of human existence, i.e. *the true Self as the ground of human existence*. 'A' stands for 'Standing on the standpoint of *A*ll Mankind', referring to the breadth of human existence, i.e. *humankind as a totality*. And 'S' stands for 'creating history *S*uprahistorically', referring to the dimension of the chronological length of human existence, i.e. *awakened human history*. Accordingly, the three aspects of FAS indicate a threefold structure of human existence, that is, depth, breadth and length of human existence, or, more concretely speaking, self, world, and history. (This threefold notion may seem to correspond to the traditional Western threefold notion, the soul, the world, and God. However, in Hisamatsu's threefold notion God is absent.) In the notion of FAS, these three dimensions of human existence are grasped dynamically, and though different from each other they are inseparably united with each other.

The first dimension, that is, 'F', which stands for 'Awakening to the *F*ormless Self', signifies nothing other than *satori* in the Zen sense. Traditionally, it has been said that the primary concern of Zen is *koji-kyūmei*, 'investigation of self', that is, to inquire into and awaken to one's own true Self, or original face. Hisamatsu calls this true Self the 'Formless Self'[9] because, being entirely unobjectifiable, true Self is without any form which can be objectified. True Self is realised as really formless by going beyond both form (being) and formlessness (non-being). Traditional Zen greatly emphasises the importance of investigating and seeing into the Self, but it also admonishes not to remain in silent illumination or fall into a nihilistic ghostly cave by attaching to the formlessness of the self. Zen thus stresses the necessity of great dynamism or the wondrous activity of helping others. Hisamatsu, however, criticises this formulation of traditional Zen by saying that if the so-called the 'wondrous activity' signifies only the process of leading other individuals to awaken to their true Self, its activity remains limited to the problem of self without penetrating more widely beyond it even by one step. He says:

> If, as has been the case with traditional Zen, [wondrous] activity starts and ends only with the so-called practice of compassion involved in helping others to awaken; such activity will remain unrelated to the formation of the world and creation of history, isolated from the world and history, and in the end turn Zen into a forest Buddhism, a temple Buddhism, at best, a Zen monastery Buddhism. Ultimately, this becomes 'Zen within a ghostly cave'.[10]

Thus, in Hisamatsu's view Buddhist compassion cannot simply be limited to helping other beings solve their religious problem. Rather the compassion of the awakened Self must entail commitment to the social-political sphere of human history as well.

> In Zen, the all-out compassionate practice ought to be to have man awake to his original true Self, that is, to the solitarily emancipated, non-dependent, Formless Self, who will form the true world and create true history self-abidingly, without being bound or fettered by anything.[11]

According to Hisamatsu, a formation of the true world necessitates the second dimension of human existence, that is 'A', which signifies 'Standing on the standpoint of *A*ll mankind'. For, unless we grasp racial, national, and class problems from the perspective of all humankind, we cannot solve any of them adequately. Thus, in addition to the 'investigation of Self', *sekai-kyūmei*, or the 'investigation of the world', is needed to find out the nature and structure of the world. Furthermore, creation of true history requires the third dimension of human existence, that is 'S', which stands for 'Creating history *S*uprahistorically', because true history cannot be created by an approach that is simply immanent in history, such as class struggle in Marxism or social reform in humanism. Unless we take as our basis a suprahistorical religious standpoint, which in Hisamatsu's case is the awakening to the formless Self, we cannot create true history. Thus *rekishi-kyūmei*,[12] or the 'investigation of history' is necessary to break through the contradiction of history, to understand the real meaning of history, and to grasp its origin and purpose.

Currently, we have different peace movements, human rights movements, and various other social reform movements. However, if these movements are pursued only from a political and social standpoint without a basis in our deep realisation of the true Self, such approaches may not yield adequate solutions. Even where those who participate in such movements are full of much good will and possess a strong sense of justice, if they lack an awakening to the original nature of self and others, their actions are without real power—or worse—create other confusions. On the other hand, if only the internal religious aspect of the human being is emphasised and priority is given to one's own salvation to the neglect of the affairs of the world, however serious an individual may be in his religious quest, he cannot attain a profound religious solution. Mere concern with self-salvation is contrary to the Bodhisattva's 'Four Great Vows'; nevertheless, contemporary Buddhism is apt to be removed from social realities, confined to temples, and engrossed only in the inner problems of the self.

Thus, together with his group of disciples, Hisamatsu formulated 'The Vow of Mankind' and proclaimed it publicly in 1951, shortly after the Korean War. 'The Vow of Mankind' reads as follows:

> Keeping calm and composed, let us awaken to our true self, become fully compassionate humans, make full use of our gifts according to our respective vocations in life; discern the agony both individual and social and its source, recognise the right direction in which history should proceed, and join hands without distinction of race, nation, or class. Let us, with compassion, vow to bring to realisation mankind's deep desire for self-emancipation and construct a world in which everyone can truly and fully live.

Koji-kyūmei, the 'investigation of self', will necessarily become abstract and without reality if it is sought only for its own sake. Therefore, we should work upon *sekai-kyūmei*, the 'investigation of the world', that is, the problem of what is the true world, what is the root and source of the world in which we live. Accordingly, the 'investigation of the world' is not separate from the 'investigation of self'. Further, to study and clarify what the world is, also is inseparably linked with *rekishi-kyūmei*, the 'investigation of history', that is, studying and clarifying the origin and true meaning of history.

In short, the question of what the self is, what the world is, and what history is, are all interrelated. The problem of what the self is cannot be resolved in its true sense if it is investigated independently of the problems of the nature of the world and the meaning of history. On the other hand, world peace, for example, cannot be established in the true sense, nor can history be truly created, unless one clarifies what the self is. These three problems are inseparably related and united at the root of our existence.

Hisamatsu thus emphasises as follows:

Without the Self-Awakening of the Formless Self, world-formation and history-creation will miss their fundamental subject. Without true formation of the world and creation of history, the Formless Self cannot help ending in an imperfect practice of compassion.

Consequently, we may conclude that we should get rid of the imperfect narrow character of the former so-called 'Self-awakened, others-awakening' activity, which disregards the world and history, and which satisfies itself at best by 'hammering out only a piece or half a piece'.[13] We should awake to the Formless Self (F), form the world on the standpoint of All mankind (A), and, without being fettered by created history, *S*uprahistorically created history at all times (S)—that is to say, only the realisation of FAS can be really called the ultimate Mahayana.[14]

Hisamatsu's notion of FAS is a remarkable example of a new understanding of transformation in contemporary Buddhism.

VI

In the preceding, I have been discussing the 'transformation in Buddhism' based upon the fundamental standpoint of Buddhism, mainly by referring to early Buddhism, to the typical form of Mahayana Buddhism, and to Zen. In

Mahayana Buddhism as it developed in China and Japan, however, there are special forms which are significantly different in their understanding of human being, death, karma, and salvation from the forms of Buddhism discussed above. The most important and conspicuous example of these types of Buddhism is Pure Land Buddhism, especially *Jōdoshinshu* founded by Shinran (1173–1263). In order to clarify the issue of 'transformation in Buddhism' more comprehensively, I now turn to *Bōdoshinshu* and to the understanding of transformation which it puts forward.

Pure Land Buddhism developed out of the original Buddhism of India and finally reached the form known as *Jōdoshinshu*. Shinran developed this reformed sect of Buddhism through a keen historical awareness of the degenerate age of the Dharma (Buddhist teaching) and a clear existential realisation of sinfulness. A prevalent historical belief among Mahayana Buddhists is a gradual degeneration of the Buddhist Dharma in three periods. According to this view, the first period of 500 or 1000 years following the Buddha's death, is called sōbō—the period of the right Dharma, in which Buddhist doctrine, practices, and enlightenment *all exist*; the second period of 500 or 1000 years is the period of Zōbō—the 'semblance' or imitative Dharma, in which doctrine and practices *exist without enlightenment*; the third and last period of 10,000 years is that of (*mappō*)—the latter or final Dharma, in which *only the doctrine remains* without practice and enlightenment. As the advent of *mappō* was perceived as increasingly imminent, many Buddhists in China and Japan turned from original Buddhism ('the right Dharma') to Pure Land Buddhism, which advocates the salvation of wretched people through faith in Amida Buddha—as the Buddhism most suitable for the *mappō* period. This historical awareness of the degeneration of Buddhist Dharma was very strong in the Kamakura Period (1185–1333) in Japan, the time in which Shinran and his teacher Hōnen were alive. Such historical awareness of the degeneration period is inseparably linked with the existential realisation of one's helplessness and sinfulness. Shan-tao (613–681), a Chinese Pure Land patriarch, on whom both Hōnen and Shinran deeply depended in their understanding of Pure Land teaching, sincerely believed and confessed that 'Being a sinful, living-dying unenlightened existence I have been incessantly transmigrated ever since the countless remote kalpa (aeons) without a single opportunity of emancipation'.[15]

For Pure Land Buddhists, the beginningless and endless process of living-dying is realised not only as karma, but also as *sinful* karma (*Zaigo*). This is because: (1) it is only by the power of Amida's *original vow to save all beings* that wretched and powerless people living in the period of degenerated Dharma can be saved; and (2) the beginningless and endless transmigration is the result of one's *unbelief* in the saving power of Amida's original vow, *that is sin.* Unlike original Buddhism, and some forms of Mahayana Buddhism, including Zen, in which a central, personal Buddha is absent, Pure Land Buddhism centres in Amida Buddha as the Buddha of infinite light and infinite life whose original vow to save *all sentient beings* is believed to be *unconditional.* Accordingly, transformation in Pure Land Buddhism is not conceivable without Amida's original vow and beneficence.

Transformation in Pure Land Buddhism is called *ōjō*, born in the Pure Land. It implies going to and being reborn in the Pure Land after death in this present defiled world. For Pure Land Buddhists, it is impossible to attain nirvana in the midst of samsara right here, right now in this actual world as most forms of Mahayana Buddhism insist. On the basis of Pure Land scriptures, especially the *Larger Sukhāvatī-vyūha-sūtra*, Pure Land Buddhists believe that in infinite time in the past the Bodhisattva Dharmākara observed the sufferings of mortal beings in the future, and, out of his great compassion, vowed to establish a land of bliss wherein all beings could be emancipated from their sufferings. After labour and meditation for long aeons, Bodhisattva Dharmākara accomplished his vow completely and became a Buddha named Amitābha or Amitāyus, residing in the Pure Land established by himself. It is a basic belief of Pure Land Buddhism that not by one's own practice and meditation, but by reciting the name of Amida (*nembutsu*), through pure faith in the saving power of Amida's vow, regardless of whether the human being's activities are good or bad; *all beings without exception can be saved* and will be reborn in the Pure Land after death.

It is Shinran who radicalised this Pure Land faith and brought it to its final conclusion. Shinran's unique standpoint may be summarised in the following three points:

First, Shinran radicalised the Pure Land teaching of universal salvation by Amida's vow regardless of one's good or evil, and emphasised that evil persons were in fact outstanding candidates for Amida's salvation.

While Hōnen, Shinran's direct teacher, stated:

> Even an evil person is born in the Pure Land, how much more so is a good person,[16]

Shinran declared:

> Even a good person is born in the Pure Land, how much more so is an evil person.[17]

To explain the reason for his position Shinran says:

> Since a man who does deeds of merit by his own effort lacks total reliance

on the Other Power, he is self-excluded from Amida's Original Vow.—It was solely to enable the wicked to attain Buddhahood that Amida took his vows, out of compassion for those like us who, defiled to the core, have no hope of liberating ourselves from the cycle of births and deaths through any other discipline. And so an evil man who dedicates himself to the Other Power is above all endowed with the right cause for Rebirth.[18]

Second, Pure Land teaching rejects various forms of Buddhist practice as invalid for one's salvation, and advocates as the way of salvation the *nembutsu*, that is, recitation of the name of Amida through faith. Shinran, however, radicalised this Pure Land teaching and rejected even the recitation of *nembutsu* as a remainder of human practice (self-power) and emphasised the single *nembutsu* in pure faith or *pure faith alone* even before uttering *nembutsu*, as a necessary and sufficient requirement of one's salvation. While Hōnen stated his position as *Nembutsu ihon*, 'the nembutsu is the foundation of salvation' Shinran advocated his position as *Shinjin ihon*, 'faith is the foundation of salvation'. For Shinran, one can be truly saved only through pure faith in the absolute other power of Amida's original vow and the *nembutsu* is not a requirement of, but an *expression of gratitude* for, the salvation that comes through the *unconditional mercy* of Amida Buddha.

Third, Shinran emphasised *Sokutokuōjō*, 'the immediate attainment of rebirth' in this actual world rather than rebirth in the Pure Land after death.

In his writing, *Yuishinshōmoni*, Shinran stated:

> *Sokutokuōjō* means that since one attains faith, therefore he is reborn. 'Therefore he is reborn' means that he abides in the state of non-retrogression. To abide in the state of non-retrogression means, namely, that it is determined that one is in the rank of the company of the truly assured. It is also called *Jōtōshōkaku*, 'to be in the state equivalent to right enlightenment'.[19]

Accordingly, as often pointed out, we see a great affinity between Shinran's *Jōdoshinshu* and Christianity, especially as represented by Paul and Luther. But we must also pay due attention to the subtle differences between them.

First, although both *Jōdoshinshu* (Shinran) and Christianity (Paul and Luther) emphasise faith alone for salvation, in Christianity it is faith in the death and resurrection of Jesus Christ as the revelation of God's redemptive love, which is definitely *historical event*; while in *Jōdoshinshu* it is faith in the original vow of Amida Buddha to save all beings, which is *transhistorical reality*.

Second, both Christianity and *Jōdoshinshu* focus on one deity, that is, Jesus

Christ and Amida Buddha respectively, but Jesus Christ is the incarnation through *kenosis* of the second person of the Trinity. His root and source is God the Father, who defines himself as 'I am that I am', *'ehyeh 'asher 'ehyeh ('hayah'* as the root of *'ehyeh'* means to become, to work, and to happen). On the other hand, Amida Buddha is a personal manifestation of Dharmakāya (the Body of Truth or *Buddha nature* itself) which is without form and without colour—a personal revelation of Sunyata (Emptiness) through its self-emptying nature.

Third, both Christianity and Jōdoshinshu emphasise *salvation in this actual world*—Paul says 'though our outward man is decaying, yet our inward man is renewed day by day' (2 Cor. 4:16) and Shinran's emphasis of *Sokutokuōjō*, immediate attainment of rebirth. However, in Christianity one's resurrection is ultimately an eschatological event which will happen at the end of history, but in *Jōdoshinshu* the fulfilment of one's rebirth is not an eschatological event but is realised after each one's death.

These three points would bear further discussion; but in brief: as compared with Christianity *Jōdoshinshu* is less future-oriented and more (absolute) present-oriented because of Amida's transhistorical character. This distinction implies an important difference in the understanding of transformation in these two religions.

Notes

1. Dōgen: the fascicle of *Shōji* in *Shōbōgenzō*. See 'Shōji' (Birth and Death), translated by Norman Waddell and Masao Abe, *Eastern Buddhist*, Vol. V. No. 1, p. 79.
2. Samyutta-nikāya, ii. 178f.
3. Masao Abe, 'Kenotic God and Dynamic Sunyata' unpublished p. 57f.
4. *Denshihōyō*. Taisho 48. No. 2012.
5. *Mumonkan*. Case 47. Taisho 48. No. 2005.
6. *Shōdaijōron. Mahāyāna-samgraha*. Taisho 31. No. 1594.
7. Masao Abe, 'Hisamatsu Shin'ichi: 1889–1980', *Eastern Buddhist*, Vol. XIV. No. 1, pp. 142–149.
8. Masao Abe, 'Hisamatsu's Philosophy of Awakening', *Eastern Buddhist*, Vol. XIV. No. 1, pp. 26–42.
9. Shin'ichi Hisamatsu, *Zen and the Fine Arts*, Kodansha International, Tokyo 1975, pp. 45–52. See also Shin'ichi Hisamatsu, 'Ultimate Crisis and Resurrection', II. *Eastern Buddhist*, Vol. VIII. No. 2, p. 62.
10. Shin'ichi Hisamatsu, 'Ultimate Crisis and Resurrection', p. 64.
11. Ibid. p. 64–65.
12. *Sekai-kyūmei* and *rekishi-kyūmei* are Abe's terms. See Masao Abe, 'A History of FAS Zen Society', *FAS Newsletter*, Autumn 1984, pp. 1–12.

13. A Zen set phrase often indicating the role of Zen master who should bring up at least a small number of enlightened disciples throughout his life.

14. Shin'ichi Hisamatsu, 'Ultimate Crisis and Resurrection', p. 65.

15. See *The Shinshu Seiten*, published by the Honpa Hongwanji Mission of Hawaii. (Tokyo: Kenkyusha 1955) p. 150.

16, 17. *The Tanni Shō* trans. Ryūkoku Translation Center Kyoto, 1966 p. 22.

18. Ibid. p. 23.

19. *Shinshū Shōgyo Zensho*. (Kyoto: Kokyo Shoin 1953) Vol. II, p. 625.

Schalom Ben-Chorin

Did God make anything happen in Christianity?

An Attempt at a Jewish Theology of Christianity

(*Paper given to the Evangelical/Catholic Clergy Day in the Diocese of Aix and Guest Lecture in the University of Munich 21.6.1982*)

IN 1889 John Wilkinson, the founder of the Mildmay Jewish Mission in London, published his book *Israel my Glory*. After the Second World War it reappeared in a German edition in Switzerland under the title *Was hat God mit den Juden vor?* and became more widely known.

From a Christian fundamentalist viewpoint the author tried to elucidate from scripture God's plan with his covenanted people Israel. Responses from the Jewish side were more negative than positive, although Wilkinson spoke so insistently, well before Theodor Herzl, about the Jews' return to their historic homeland, Palestine, the land of Israel. Any attempt from outside to interpret God's ways with his people Israel was and is regarded by Jews as presumptuous interference.

And now you ask me the question: 'Did God make anything happen in Christianity?' You expect me to try to offer you a Jewish theology of Christianity—that is, a Jewish reply to the Church's challenge to Judaism.

I can imagine there are many Christians who would regard it as presumptuous and out of order for me to attempt to answer this question, because for Christians, it is clear that in Christianity—that is in the person of Jesus Christ—God's self-revelation to the world attained its culmination. As *Hebrews* expresses in it in its introductory formula: 'In many and various ways

God spoke of old to our fathers by the prophets; but in these last days he has spoken to us by a Son, whom he appointed the heir of all things, through whom also he created the world. ...'

If Christians know this, isn't it out of order to ask whether God made anything happen in Christianity? I would not dare put such a question to a Christian but since a Christian has asked me the question, I shall not evade it and must try to answer it.

A Christian theologian of our time, Helmut Gollwitzer, spoke clearly on this subject: 'For the Jewish faith nothing essential changed in the world with Jesus; for Christian faith Jesus is the decisive break in world history; although the world appears to go on just the same, nevertheless everything has changed. Here everything seems to support the Jewish view; the Christian view is much less believable and much harder for us all to understand.'[1]

I could not put it more clearly than that. In fact, for Jewish faith the appearance of Jesus does not mean that God made that change happen which Jews look forward to in their messianic hope. In the Christmas Gospel Jesus' birth is heralded by angels singing (Luke 2:14). 'Glory to God in the highest and on earth peace among men with whom he is pleased.'

Two thousand years later, where is this peace of God? The world is rocked by war and hatred, holocaust, nuclear threat, racism, class hatred, quarrelling, envy and covetousness. This is not renewal. According to the Christian faith Jesus' sacrifice on Golgotha brought about the reconciliation between God and sinful humanity 'for God so loved the world that he gave his only son ...' (John 3:16).

But how has God's sacrificial love produced any effect in the actual world? John's Gospel continues in the next verse: 'For God sent the Son into the world, not to condemn the world, but that the world might be saved through him.'

So where is this saved world? What does it look like? Has the world changed in any fundamental way since the birth of Christ? The Christian can only answer this question by turning inwards and by exchatological hope, through John's axiom: 'He who believes in him (Jesus) is not condemned; he who does not believe in him is condemned already because he has not believed in the name of the only Son of God.' In almost two thousand years of Christianity, the proof of this cool assertion has not been forthcoming.

In accordance with the prophetic message, Judaism awaits a visible change in history through God's messianic coming:

'They shall beat their swords into ploughshares,
and their spears into pruning hooks;
nation shall not lift up sword against nation,

neither shall they learn war any more;
but they shall sit every man under his vine and under his fig tree,
and none shall make them afraid.' (Mic. 4:3; Isa. 2:4)

Where is this redeemed world and the redeemed creatures of whom Isaiah speaks?

'The wolf shall dwell with the lamb,
and the leopard shall lie down with the kid,
and the calf and the lion and the fatling together,
and a little child shall lead them.' (Isa. 11:16)

None of this actually happened with the birth and death of Jesus of Nazareth. So has nothing really changed? Of course there have always been Jews who have reacted as negatively as Novalis, himself a Christian, did in a different context: 'Christianity is an illusion.'

However this denial of salvation history elements in Christianity by Judaism strikes me as untenable. Here I should like to start from Rabban Gamaliel's speech in the Council reported in *Acts* 5:34–39: 'But a Pharisee in the Council named Gamaliel, a teacher of the Law, held in honour by all the people, stood up and ordered the men to be put outside for a while. And he said to them, "Men of Israel, take care what you do with these men. For before these days Theudas arose, giving himself out to be somebody, and a number of men, about four hundred, joined him; but he was slain and all who followed him were dispersed and came to nothing. After him Judas the Galilean arose in the days of the census and drew away some of the people after him; he also perished, and all who followed him were scattered. So in the present case I tell you, keep away from these men and let them alone; for if this plan or this undertaking is of men, it will fail; but if it is of God, you will not be able to overthrow them. You might even be found opposing God!" So they took his advice ...'

The Gamaliel mentioned here is given the name Rabban Gamaliel in the *Mishna* and was the apostle Paul's teacher. His speech given here is not entirely accurate historically, because the Theudas mentioned had not yet appeared. Flavius Josephus mentions him in his *Jewish Antiquities* 22:5:1 as a 'prophet', who arose in the Forties under the procurator Cuspius Fadus and tried to lead his disciples dry-footed through the Jordan. He was executed by the Romans. In Gamaliel's speech given in *Acts* this Theudas comes before the Judas who appeared in 7 AD. As Gamaliel must have given his speech before 44, the year of Theudas' death, this part as reported in *Acts* cannot be right.

However this is no reason to dismiss the speech and its core theology of history: judgment by historical results.

Judaism and Christianity are historical religions in contrast to pagan nature myths. God is seen not only as the creator of the world but also as the lord of history. And so history must show traces of God. In the Jewish view history is always also seen as salvation history. And now Judaism must recognise that the messianic movement that began with Jesus of Nazareth, unlike the thirty or so other messianic movements from Bar-Kochba to Sabbatai Zewi, did not remain just an episode but endured throughout history.

Here we may quote Jesus' parable of the grain of mustard seed: 'He said, "With what can we compare the kingdom of God or what parable shall we use for it? It is like a grain of mustard seed, which, when sown upon the ground, is the smallest of all the seeds on earth; and yet when it is sown it grows up and becomes the greatest of all shrubs, and *puts forth large branches* so that *the birds of the air can make their nests in its shade."* ' (Mark 4:30–32)

Even if we don't call it the kingdom of God we have to admit that the Church has grown from the tiny mustard seed of the primitive Christian community into the huge tree overshadowing the world. Can this have happened without God having a hand in it?

Even early medieval Jewish authorities stressed Jesus' historical results. In his classical work *Jesus of Nazareth* (Berlin 1930) Joseph Klausner remarks: 'So what is Jesus for the Jews of our time?'

From a human point of view he is certainly a 'light of nations'. His disciples spread the teaching of Israel, even though in garbled and imperfect form, among pagans in all parts of the earth. No Jew can deny this world historical significance of Jesus and his teaching. And in fact neither Maimonides nor Jehuda Halevi overlooked it.

Maimonides (1135–1204) described Jesus as the 'waymaker for the Messiah King.' This disputed formula is found in Maimonides' compendium *Mishna Thora Hilchoth Melakhim* 11:4, according to older uncensored versions. Klausner quotes it in full in the original Hebrew edition of his work (Tel Aviv, 1945) p. 519.

Jehuda Halevi (1080–1145) speaks similarly in his dialogue book *Kusari*, in which a Jew, a Christian and a Moslem explain the elements of their faith to the King of the Chazars.

In his commentary *Beth Habechira* on the Talmud treatise *Aboda Sara* the Provençal Jew Menachem Meiri (1242–1306) also describes Christians (and Moslems) as 'people distinguished by the ways of faith'. In this connection Robert Raphael Geis[2] remarked: 'Meiri is of the opinion that in his time idolatry had almost completely disappeared. He ascribes to Christians and Mohammedans knowledge of God and faith in his existence, oneness and power, "even though they misunderstand many things in our faith" ' (*Beth Habechira* on *Gittin* p. 246). Thus according to Meiri the Christian is like the Ger Torschav, proselytes without full status of Talmudic times (*Beth Habechira* on *Aboda Sara* p. 214), who partly adopted Jewish teaching and the Jewish way of life. This idea is frequently taken up or developed by Rabbinic scholars in the middle ages.

Not all Rabbinic authorities in the Jewish middle ages, which lasted considerably longer than the European, shared this view. There were also sharp rejections of Christianity. We may mention Joseph Albo, who wrote in Spain in the first decades of the fifteenth century, and in his major dogmatic work *Sepher Ha Ikkarim* accused New Testament sources of defective knowledge of the Hebrew bible, because in the Gospels and the Acts of the Apostles, verses from the Old Testament are ripped out of context and misquoted.

In his study of theological disputes between Jews and Christians in the Iberian Peninsula Hans Georg von Mutius remarks: 'The polemic that our author (Joseph Albo) engages in to attack the New Testament is on the one hand very powerful. On the other hand we should not forget that it occurs in an apologetic context. Apologists are not interested in the question of truth as such. His purpose is to use his sharp intellect to cut his opponent's world view to pieces. The truth of his own tradition is held *a priori* to be beyond doubt. This is the point at which we can become critical. He attacks the quotations in Matthew's Gospel purporting to show prophecies have been fulfilled on the grounds that they have been taken out of their factual and literary context. But the same could be said about the Talmud and the Midrash literature, whose biblical exegesis is just as arbitrary. If Joseph Albo had judged rabbinic literature by the same standards he used to condemn the New Testament with, he would have had to condemn it too. However he completely overlooked this and probably was not even aware he was being illogical. Because of the total critical hostility to Judaism in the surrounding Christian world, critical questions by Jews about their own tradition simply did not arise.'[3] What has been said here about Albo could be said about many Jewish writers before the Enlightenment. Christian triumphalism pushed Jews into a defensive position, which made it difficult or impossible for them to recognise the positive and common features Christianity shared with Judaism. Jews were constantly threatened with forced baptism, banishment and death. This made it difficult for them to make objective judgments about the New Testament and Christianity.

Ecclesia militans, the fighting Church, drove Jews into a defensive position which affected their attitude to the Church. It therefore achieved the opposite effect to the one intended. Because of the Church's aggression it was impossible for Jews to see that God did make something happen in Christianity, a *drawing nearer* of the goal of history, the kingdom of God.

Of course from the Jewish point of view what Christianity claims to have happened has not happened. Thus we find this footnote to Matthew 27:51b–53: 'The earth shook, and the rocks were split; the tombs also were opened and many bodies of the saints who had fallen asleep were raised.'

The footnote reads: 'These events indicate that with Jesus' death and resurrection the power of death is broken.' (*New Testament.* Common Translation (into German) of Holy Scripture. 2nd revised edition Stuttgart 1980).

The theological axiom that through Jesus' death and resurrection the power of death was broken does not correspond in any way to the facts. People died before and after Jesus' death and resurrection. The world's infrastructure has not been changed by it. Even if we accept Jesus' resurrection as a completed act of salvation, this does not mean a conquest of death for human beings. The doctrine of the two natures propounds that the divine in Jesus achieved *its* overcoming of death, whereas we mortals, who only have one nature, have not yet been included in the proclaimed conquest of death. This great promise of a salvation already dawned Judaism has rejected as an illusion.

Nevertheless in Christianity God did make something happen, which Jewish realism cannot overlook. In every generation of Christians there have been people whose faces were like soft wax stamped with the seal of Christ. In all their diversity many Christians were stamped with Christ's seal, among others, Francis of Assisi, Tolstoy, Kierkegaard, Albert Schweitzer, Dietrich Bonhoeffer to Mother Theresa in our own time. Although these people were all very different, they all experienced what Paul expressed in these words: 'If we live, we live to the Lord, and if we die we die to the Lord; so then, whether we live or whether we die, we are the Lord's' (Rom. 14:18).

No other historical figure has stamped others in this way. The person of Jesus, about whom we know relatively little, has transformed the image of humanity, not all of them of course, but many individuals, who did not act on their own from their experience of their encounter with Jesus.

From the Jewish point of view we can say that though the kingdom of God did not dawn with Jesus of Nazareth, nevertheless a 'cloud of witnesses' arose, who by following Jesus set out on the way to God's kingdom. The Frankfurt New Testament scholar, Hans Werner Bartsch formulated in thus: 'In Jesus of Nazareth I see Jahweh's arm outstretched to the nations.' As a Jew I can agree with this formula. Bartsch could hardly have said what he did had not the way been prepared by Franz Rosenzweig seven decades earlier. In a letter to Rudolf Ehrenberg written on 1 November 1913 Rosenzweig writes: 'No one *comes* to the Father—except someone who no longer needs to come to the

Father because he is already with him. And this is the case with the people of Israel (not individual Jews). The people of Israel, chosen by the Father, stare out over the world and history to that far off final point where this same Father, the one and only one, will be All in All.'[4]

This often quoted sentence of Rosenzweig's is not of course exegetically tenable. For John's Jesus says this is a dispute with the Jews and Paul expressly stresses that the gospel was to be preached *first* to the Jews and then *also* to the Greeks. *From a Christian viewpoint* Rosenzweig's distinction between *coming* and *being* does not hold. Nevertheless this is a legitimate insight *from Jewish experience*. But even if we say that Jesus showed the Gentiles the way to the Father, because for them he *is* the way, this is still not the last word on the meaning of Jesus for Judaism.

Modern Jewish theologians, especially those belonging to the Liberal Reform, have expressly suggested that Jesus, the New Testament and therefore Christianity, can also contribute to the elucidation of Judaism. Thus Rabbi Leo Baeck calls the Gospel a 'proclamation of the Jewish history of faith'. Rabbi Maurice Eisendrath, President of the Union of American Hebrew Congregations, stressed at a conference of this organisation of North American Jewish Reform communities in the Sixties, that we as Jews can learn from Jesus' ethical stance. And a generation earlier the leader of Liberal Judaism in England, Claude Montefiore, set Jesus's ethics above that of the Rabbis, which provoked furious disagreement from the Hebrew culture philosopher Achad Haam.

In retrospect we can see that religious impulses from Jesus' person and message permeate Judaism today. Returning to your question I should like to say that a lot more was made to happen by God in Jesus of Nazareth than in the works of the Church and Christianity. We can illustrate this from the dialectic of Christianity. Christianity conquered when it was defeated (on the Cross) and was defeated when it conquered (after Constantine).

Let us oppose these two symbols of victory in defeat and defeat in victory, the Cross and the so-called Christ monogram. The Cross shows the shuddering horror of a Jew who knows himself to be completely one with the divine Father and in his martyrdom cries out with the words of the psalm: 'My God, my God, why have you forsaken me?' His disciples however were certain that this was not the last word and so for believers the death on the Cross is lit by the light of Easter morning. Defeat turns to victory.

According to legend the Christ monogram appeared to the Roman Emperor Constantine (274–337) in a dream before his decisive battle with his rival Maxentius (324) and told him he would win: *hoc signo vinces* (in this sign you will conquer). Constantine took it as his *labarum*, the standard for his legions. The monogam actually expresses the defeat of Christianity, which henceforth became a state religion and, among other things, persecuted the Jews. The beatitude proclaiming, 'Blessed are the persecuted', was forgotten. Christians were the bloodiest persecutors of the Jews. In this development we can see the victory of the devil's power over the divine, expressed by the Swiss historian Jakob Burkhardt in the words: 'Power makes people evil.' When Christianity became powerful we no longer see God's rule, rather that of his Adversary. However nowadays the thick fog is lifting from the landscape on whose horizon we can see the kingdom of God. The Church is no longer powerful and therefore it can become the vessel of the Holy Spirit again. In powerlessness Judaism and Christianity meet, perhaps for the first time in history.

At the beginning of Christianity Jesus' disciples were pursued by the hatred of the Jews. Centuries later the Christians—completely against their master's teaching—repaid a thousandfold what Jews had done to them in earlier times. Two thousand years had to go by before Jews and Christians could meet no longer as persecutor and persecuted but as brothers at a moment when materialism in both East and West threatened their faith and therefore believers. Jews and Christians were drawn together by necessity. Can we in faith explain this as other than something done by God? I'd like to call this happening brough about by God as the *reuniting of God's scattered people*.

The people of God were thought of in the first place as an ethnic plurality as we see from the call of Abraham: 'I will make of you a great nation, and I will bless you and make your name great, so that you will be a blessing. I will bless those who bless you, and him who curses you I will curse; and in you all the families of the earth will be blessed.' (Gen. 1:2-4) If we look more closely at this blessing given to Abraham at his calling, we see clearly that in this great people 'all the families of the earth' will be united in one blessed community.

What we see coming today if we follow the signs of the times, is an ecumenical gathering of Abraham's children, Jews, Christians and Muslims together. Jews and Arabs (the bearers of Islam) are the genetic descendants of Abraham and Christians are the spiritual children of the Father of Faith, as Paul said. The reuniting of the divided people of God is the great task for the future. For nearly two thousands years a false and fatal alternative was presented: either Jews or the Church are God's people.

The Church proclaimed itself as the New Israel and denied ancient Israel, Judaism, any relevance to the history of salvation. The Church saw itself as Israel's heir, whereas the apostle Paul rated pagan Christians only as co-heirs of the promise.

The Jews saw the Christians, who were now the overwhelming majority surrounding the old Israel, as 'Goyim', pagans, who in Talmudic times were idolators and star-worshippers and therefore totally disqualified.

The Church did not see the covenant made to the old Israel and Judaism did not see that the God of Israel had revealed himself in Christianity. Of course the Christians began by saying solemnly of Jesus:

'For he is our peace, who has made us both one and has broken down the dividing wall of hostility, by abolishing in his flesh the law of commandments and ordinances, that he might create in himself one new man in place of the two, so making peace, and might reconcile us both to God in one body through the Cross, thereby bringing the hostility to an end. And he came and preached peace to you who were far off and peace to those who were near; for through him we both have access in one Spirit to the Father. So then you are no longer strangers and sojourners, but you are fellow citizens with the saints and members of the household of God.' (Eph. 2:14–19).

However Church history made a mockery of this apostolic proclamation of peace. The Church's Christ did not do away with the enmity but deepened it. The Cross of reconciliation became the Cross of persecution. The Church therefore needs to re-read its own sacred texts.

But Judaism must also come to a new understanding of its prophetic tradition. Thus the synagogue takes as a prophetic insight into the Genesis story of the call of Abraham quoted above part of Chapter 37 of the book of Ezekiel: 'The word of the Lord came to me: "Son of man, take a stick and write on it, 'For Judah and the children of Israel associated with him'; then take another stick and write upon it, 'For Joseph (the stick of Ephraim) and all the house of Israel associated with him'; and join them together into one stick, that they may become one in your hand." ' (Ezek. 37:15–17)

This symbolic action by the prophet is supposed to show the reuniting of Israel and Judah. Would it not be appropriate to carry over this process of reunification of the divided people of God into our own situation. Now the two sections of the people of God needing to be reunited are Judaism and Christianity.

Can there be two chosen people? As we said, this question has for centuries driven the Church to take a wrong attitude towards the Jews. According to Rauschning this question also drove Adolf Hitler to his position. He regarded the Germans as the chosen people and therefore wanted the Jews to be annihilated. This horrendous mistake led to the sacrifice of millions of lives.

Can there be two chosen peoples? No. There is only one people of God but it consists of several parts. This was true in ancient Israel with the twelve tribes and these were the foundation of greater Israel consisting of all who professed the God of Abraham, Isaac and Jacob.

Both prophet and apostle speak of wood reunited. 'Wood' and 'tree' are the same word in Hebrew, 'ejz' and thus the Torah, God's Word, is shown as the 'tree of life'. 'She is the tree of life to those who lay hold of her; those who hold her fast are called happy.' (Prov. 3:18).

If we get away from the big stick with which we have historically beaten each other, to the tree of life of salvation history, we will see clearly that in Christianity God made something happen and that in Judaism God is still making things happen.

Translated by Dinah Livingstone

Notes

1. H. Gollwitzer/P. Lapide *Ein Fluchtlingskind (Auslegung zu Luk. 2* (Munich 1981) Kiaser-Traktate no. 63, p. 44.
2. R. Geis 'Zum Problem gemeinsamer christlich-jüdischer Gottesdienste', *Einladung ins Lehrhaus*. Arnoldshainer Texte. (1981).
3. Hans-Georg von Mutius 'Die Beurteilung Jesu und des Neuen Testaments beim spanisch-jüdischen Religionsphilosophen Josef Albo', *Freiburger Zeitschrift für Philosophie und Theologie*, vol. 27, no. 3 (1980).
4. Franz Rosenzweig *Briefe* (Berlin 1935) p. 73.

PART III

Christian Identity and Community Membership

Alphonse Ngindu Mushete

The Figure of Jesus in African Theology

THEOLOGY MEANS questioning and thereby theology is universal. When questioning becomes question theology must turn contextual. Then it adopts a world view, the result of a group's encounters with its environment, which ordains common modes of reaction and action, of thinking and speaking, and of feeling and being. The contemporary term for all this is 'anthropology'.

In this article I shall try to show that in Africa a Christology responsive to African history and culture is not only coming into being but developing.

Four main topics are covered:
1. The vitality of African cultures and religions;
2. continuing domination;
3. the anthropological bases of African Christology;
4. Christological language.

1. THE VITALITY OF AFRICAN CULTURES AND RELIGIONS

In spite of the colonial experience and its depersonalising system of cultural suppression and eradication, there is still a good deal of life in African cultures. This vitality is shown particularly in the renewal of African languages, plastic arts, dance, music and literature, both in Africa and in the communities of the black African diaspora.[1] The World Festival of Negro Arts at Dakar (1966) and at Lagos (1977) remains the finest expression of the lasting nature of African cultures. Their liveliness is also shown successfully in such new forms and technologies as cinema and television. It complements the African contribution in the sphere of the human sciences (anthropology, philosophy, sociology, history and so on), medicine (traditional pharmacopoeia), and the spiritual experience of humanity.[2] This cultural vitality is still the major support of the African nations in their struggle for complete liberation and for the construction of a society which can deal with contemporary problems. The final declaration of the Accra colloquium says as much in a text full of optimism and hope: 'For us, the rapid growth of the people of God in Africa, the originality of the African experience of Christian life in worship, a typically African liturgy, Bible reading and communitarian life are signs of hope and confidence'.[3]

2. CONTINUING DOMINATION

An objective analysis of the situation of the African nations in Africa and in the diaspora shows however that they are still the victims of a domination born of slavery and colonisation. Today this situation takes several forms: racism above all in South Africa; a degree of neo-colonialism everywhere; underdevelopment enhanced and to some extent provoked by economic exploitation by the great powers; and cultural imperialism masquerading under a plethora of euphemisms.[4]

This situation continues within the churches, where the model imported from the West is still imposed and accepted, and the local churches are kept in an immature condition spiritually, institutionally and materially. This state of affairs is well-known.[5]

This situation is especially evident in theological thought. The teachings imparted by missionary schools have been imposed on the life of the African churches as a theology of conversion of 'pagans', as 'foundation stones', or as stages of adaptation and implantation of the Church.[6]

3. ANTHROPOLOGICAL BASES OF AFRICAN CHRISTOLOGY

The problem of theology, it has been said, is essentially that of biblical faith expressed in a language and in categories belonging to a world view and a conception of humanity proper to a given cultural tradition. Here I must stress two major aspects which are also closely connected:
  —the biblical message is addressed to actual historical human beings situated in time and space, and carrying out their destiny in a dynamic way;
  —anthropology and cosmology as cited here define the way in which people, within a specific cultural community, understand and define themselves in relation to other people and to the world. This conception of people and the world is also dynamic.

The conception of people and of the world which emerges from the study of the artistic and religious traditions of the African nations may be summarised in a few main points, which were accurately grasped and expressed at the Accra colloquium.

1. The African remains deeply realistic in everything. He or she has a genetically established and ineradicable feeling for reality.

2. Together with this sense of reality the African has a feeling for nature. Almost instinctively, he or she has a sense of divine mystery and of divine transcendence. Consequently Africans have a sense of the sacred.[7]

3. Human destiny constitutes the foundation, purpose and contents of the cultural expressions of the African nations.

4. This destiny may be defined primarily as a dramatic conflict between life and death.

5. The conflict has but one meaning: the victory of life over death.

6. The human being is rent by the struggle between life and death, and the universe conceived in the human image, is torn by the same conflict. Therefore it is divided into two camps; one consisting of those who espouse life, and the other of the those who are on the side of death.

7. Hence human beings, taking for granted that life will prove victorious, ensure not only their own destiny but that of the world. The human being is the very microcosm at the heart of the macrocosm and assures overall unity.

8. The African man or woman also lives as a collegial being, as a bundle of interpersonal and cosmic relations. He or she is simultaneously:
—a monad—an individual and not a person,
—a dyad—man and woman, when he or she constitutes a person,
—a triad—father, mother, child, when he or she becomes family, society or community.

9. As a person, a man or woman is therefore simultaneously welded to humankind and to the world.[8]

4. A CHRISTOLOGICAL LANGUAGE

There are many important christological implications of these anthropological and cosmological findings. I shall restrict myself here to a few of them.[9]

For us Africans Christ's incarnation is not only the mystery of the divine Word made flesh but the mystery of the Son of God made man. We have to speak not only of incarnation but of humanisation or, better still, of humanification. Yet, as I have remarked, to become a human person is to become a bundle of interpersonal relations welding the human subject to the human community and to the totality of the cosmos. Understood thus, the incarnation of the Word takes up the whole of humankind and the cosmos. Christ is the Chief, the Ancestor of humankind, in the sense of African anthropology to be sure.[10] For the Luba, the people to which I belong, Christ is seen and presented in the liturgy with the characteristics of a great chief. He is called Ntita (Chief of chiefs); Luaba (chosen to rule); Cimankinda or Cilobo (Hero: he who is in the vanguard and who leads the battle lines but never runs from the enemy).

This is nicely expressed in the following prayer, taken from the missal according to the use of the diocese of Mbujimayi:

'Lord God ... help us to hear your word, the example of the Anointed, Luaba and our Chief, who conquers Satan and all evil, he who has life and power, world without end. Amen'.[11]

Then:

'Cimankinda full of life and honour, you sacrificed yourself to wipe out our sins. Enable us to do good, and then we shall be with you when you come ... Jesus the Anointed, Cilobo who never runs from the enemy, accept the offering of our faith, and take it to the Father, you who have life and power ... Amen'.[12]

The first-born among the dead, Christ appears as the Ancestor of ancestors, the Ancestor of humankind, the sole mediator between God and human beings. He is the way, the gate of entry to the Father (John 10:9). In him the mediatory words and actions of our ancestors culminate and are fulfilled. The Ancestor of Christians, Christ is the Ancestor of the Bantu ancestors. Father Nkongolo has expressed this well: 'The tribe does not live only on earth. It is divided into two parts: the living and the dead. Everything which happens to the living is always experienced by the dead too; everything is controlled together for the good of the tribe: by the living, together with the spirits of the ancestors. The spirits are the dead. They have their villages and they are alive, though differently from us. Under the earth, in the ancestors' village, everything is different from here ... As Christians, we feel very much in accord with that and do not wish to deny it. Surely it was the Ancestor of Christians himself who told us: 'I shall not leave you orphans, I shall come to you ...'. Our little spirit box should be in our church ... We should draw a tall spirit tree on the altar where mass is celebrated. Then, when we enter the church we shall think of our dead ones and honour their spirits ... The Church is the house of spirits because it is the house of the Chief of spirits, Jesus Christ'.[13]

Seen in this way, Christ is truly the Amen of the universe, the *Testis verus et fidelis*. We can never stress too much the fact that Christ did not come into this world to make speeches to us or to dictate a book to a stenographer. He came to teach people to live and to die ('Mudi kufua ne kuya moyo'). He came among us to establish a life. Contrary to what certain positivist sociologists have always tried to maintain, in establishing a life he established a community. One must result from the other. His truth from the start, as it remains today, has been the food of this life and the unifying bond of this community.[14]

This is a rich idea and it can support an entire theology of the supernatural and of grace. I shall return to this point. The process of expressing the supernatural world—that is, intimate life or Revelation—like the dogma which expresses it, is no more than a manifestation of what we are and what we should be.

Christ reveals us to ourselves. His life illumines our life decisively. That does not mean that we reject the objective nature of God's historical revelation. Not at all. Christ's revelation is not subsidiary or accidental. But we consider this revelation to be accompanied essentially by an action: that is, by the operation of grace which establishes the supernatural in us. This point has to be stressed. Christ is the Founder of the entire human order in his capacity as God-man and Man-God. Through him God binds himself to us so that, all bound together in Him, we shall be bound together to Him. Christ is the 'Cipanda wa nshindamenu', the nub on which rests and turns the entire personalist metaphysics wholly characteristic of the gospel message.

The Accra colloquium has expressed this in an especially precise text: 'The destiny of the human person and the framework of life are the basic phenomena of the life of the African people ... Human destiny is the dramatic conflict between life and death, a conflict which finds its purpose in the victory of life over death. There is unity and continuity between the destiny of the person and that of the cosmos. The victory of life in the human person is also the victory of life in the cosmos. African anthropology and cosmology are optimistic. In African theology the salvation of the human person is the salvation of the universe, and in the mystery of Christ's incarnation it comprehends the human and cosmic totalities'.[15]

That is what Christ means for us. He does not work some external revelation to bring people a truth which is alien or supplementary. He reveals people to themselves by revealing God to them. It is the truth of the human being which he teaches human beings to perceive. He does not impose it on human beings like a yoke, through an external and superior authority (for then it would no longer be a saving truth for mankind). He reveals it to people in order to illumine in them the obligation to think and live it. Here we rediscover one of the finest teachings of Vatican II: 'In reality, it is only in the mystery of the Word made flesh that the mystery of man truly becomes clear. For Adam, the first man, was a type of him who was to come, Christ the Lord, Christ the new Adam, in the very revelation of the mystery of the Father and of his love, fully reveals man to himself and brings to light his most high calling'. And again: 'He who is the "image of the invisible God" (Col. 1:15), is himself the perfect man who has restored in the children of Adam that likeness to God which had been disfigured ever since the first sin. Human nature, by the very fact that it was assumed, not absorbed in him, has been raised in us also to a dignity beyond compare. For, by his incarnation, he, the Son of God, has in a certain way united himself with each man. He worked with human hands; he thought with a human mind. He acted with a human will, and he loved with a human heart. Born of the Virgin Mary, he has truly been made one of us, like to us in all things except sin'.[16]

In this perspective, clearly, a certain Christian theology of the supernatural has to be rethought. In any hypothesis, the operative contradiction between profane and sacred between nature and supernature, is at the very least simplistic and in any case poorly established in historical and theological argumentation. In its essential meaning, the Christian supernatural is not something which is added to our 'nature' from outside, by being juxtaposed to or superimposed on it. On the contrary, it is an in-depth relationship with God and with other human beings.[17] The theology of the supernatural should start from and end at the Incarnation, or else founder.

'Jesus is therefore above all the spirits. He is our spirit (ancestor) for us because we are ... born again through baptism. We are humans but we are also of the tribe of God through our baptism. Therefore we have ancestors in two ways. The great spirit (ancestor) is always Christ, the dead and risen child of God. He is the first among the dead. After Christ we can discern other founder-spirits. First there is the Holy Virgin Mary ... Then there are the saints ... And we must not forget our own dead'—Father Nkongolo.[18]

5. CONCLUSION

The best way for me to conclude these few notes on the Christ figure in African theology is to quote the following passage, with which Mgr A. T. S. Sanon ends his excellent article on 'Jesus, master of initiation':

'... the Face of Christ is an "ancestral mask, with the clear countenance of the invisible Divine, with the unique countenance of the Servant-Chief, the everlasting Son who unites us with the gifts of the Father, the Founder of the beginnings of the world, the Master of the Word who initates human beings, the one who reveals the secrets of the Kingdom, who hears the Name of the known names of God". He comments: 'An African countenance for Christ?—Yes, on condition that we acknowledge that we are still on the threshold of a great hope. A Christology which takes into account the contribution of African traditions as homage to Christ is on its way. It will arise from the deeply Christian life of communities, and from the rich thought of theologians contemplating the Word of Life in order to translate his Countenance into the rich diversity of African symbolism'.[19]

Translated by J. G. Cumming

Notes

1. On the vitality of African cultures, see especially the work of the Centre d'Etudes de Religions Africaines (CERA) (Zaïre).
2. An illuminating work on this point is *L'Afrique et ses formes de Vie Spirituelle*, Minutes of the international colloquium at Kinshasa.
3. See *Adaptation ou libération? La théologie africaine s'interroge*. The Accra colloquium (Paris 1979). I cite this volume as 'Accra colloquium'.
4. Cf. Accra colloquium, final message, pp. 225–227.
5. Cf. the declaration of the Symposium of Episcopal Conferences of Africa and Madagascar (SCEAM): *Eglise et Promotion humaine en Afrique* (Kinshasa 1985).
6. See my contribution 'L'histoire de la théologie africaine' in Accra colloquium, pp. 30–38.
7. Cf. *Les médiations africaines du sacré*, Third international Kinshasa colloquium (Kinshasa 1987).
8. Mveng, 'L'art d'Afrique noire. Liturgie cosmique et langage religieux', in Accra colloquium, pp. 167–173.
9. There are some excellent and relevant pages in the work edited by F. Kabasele, J. Dore and R. Luneau, *Chemins de la christologie africaine* (Paris 1986).
10. See, e.g., F. Kabasele, 'Le Christ comme Chef', in *Chemins de la christologie africaine* pp 109–25; *id.*, 'Le Christ comme ancêtre et aîné, in *Chemins de la Christologie africaine*, pp. 128–141; A. T. Sanon, 'Jesus, maître d'initiation', *ibid.* pp 144–166.
11. Cf. the missal of the Mbujimayi diocese published as *Didia Mfumu* ('Meal of the Lord', Kinshasa 1980, Year C) p. 87, cf. the introit.
12. *Ibid.* pp. 123, 160. Cf. the offertories.
13. *Nkongolo wa Mbiye, 'le culte des esprits'* (Kinshasa 1974) pp 7, 20, 21.
14. This accords entirely with the best aspects of African anthropology: the sense of communitarian spirit. Cf. B. Bujo, 'Nos ancêtres, ces saints inconnus', in *Bulletin de théologie africaine* (Kinshasa) Vol. I, 2 (1979) pp. 165–178.
15. Accra colloquium, p. 230.
16. Vatican II, 'Gaudium et Spes', 22. This teaching was cited and considerably elucidated by John Paul II in the encyclical *Redemptor hominis*.
17. Cf. Accra colloquium, p. 226. Cf. especially: ' "What God expects from all creation" is that people should obey his desire for a total human community and thereby Christ's commandment should be fulfilled that he asks us to like our neighbour as ourselves'.
18. Nkongolo wa Mbiye, *Le culte des esprits*, pp. 18–20.
19. A. T. Sanon, 'Jesus, maître d'initiation'. Cf. F. Kabasele *et al.*, *Chemins de la christologie africaine*, p. 166.

Peter Eicher

The Burning Bush: Holy Scripture and the Reformation Question of Identity

'HOLY SCRIPTURE uses words better and more precisely than the prying scholastics in their studies. Anyone therefore who does not renounce their imagined conceits and does not as it were like Moses take his or her shoes off will not be able to come close to the burning bush, for "the place ... is holy ground".' With this image of the Bible as the burning bush Martin Luther placed man in the fire of God's own word right at the start of his first published work, the commentary on the psalms.[1]

Just as the messenger of Yahweh appeared to the broken and guilty Moses, so the biblical message appears to man broken and defeated in the sight of God and guilty towards his or her neighbour. And just as God himself called Moses by his name from out of the burning bush so too does scripture call by his or her own name every one to whom it is proclaimed. At the place of this 'great sight' (Exod. 3:3) the God of the fathers revealed his name and sent Moses out to liberate his people from Pharaoh. Similarly in the witness of scripture God's human word chooses itself a people in order to send it out into the world to proclaim the liberating news of God's merciful action. Only the image of the burning bush is not extraneous to the Bible, it is not any comparison drawn in from outside, rather the image comes from its inmost core. For the letters of scripture, dead in themselves, are enlisted by the voice of God to which they bear witness in order 'to seek and to save the lost': it is God's own Word as it can be grasped in human terms in the story of Jesus Christ that glows throughout the whole of scipture. In the encounter with this word man is called out of his or her misery: 'Did not our hearts burn within us while he talked to us on the road, while he opened to us the scriptures?' (Luke 24:32).

1. THE QUESTIONING OF IDENTITY BY SCRIPTURE

It is no accident that Martin Luther used the image he had merely hinted at precisely in the context of the question that later brought with it the renewal of the Reformation and thus also the permanent division of the Church into two. In Martin Luther's eyes the theologians who with their 'imagined conceits' were polluting the holy ground were the teachers of self-justification in the sight of God. They provided another foundation than the Gospel of Jesus Christ which he found celebrated already in the psalms. In his view the 'scholastics' ascribed to man summoned by the Bible the ability and the duty of being able to become just towards God and neighbour through his or her own decisions and his or her good behaviour. Thus, to put it in modern terms, the teaching of scripture would merely help man through his or her personally and socially meaningful behaviour to discover himself or herself. Scripture would be the midwife of his or her identity and the instrument of a proclamation by the Church that would be able to help the believer towards this identity. But according to Martin Luther this confidence was completely called into question and shattered by the content of scripture. As the one who is crucified and raised up, the Lord whose voice finds expression in the whole of scripture, contradicts his creature imprisoned in guilt and mortality, and does so in a way that despite appearances is good. He frees man from his or her despairing attempt to have to realise his or her own self-fulfilment.

Now in this context we are not concerned with the historical question whether with this criticism of the Erfurt scholasticism he was best acquainted with Martin Luther misunderstood the doctrine of grace of the late middle ages.[2] Rather what we are concerned with here is the factual question of the connection between the Reformation's hearkening anew to the voice of scripture and man's search for his or her identity before God and his or her fellow men and women. Right from the start the Reformation linked together awareness of the Word of God witnessed in the Bible and the questioning of every attempt at self-assertion in the face of God on the part of man and the Church. Because the content of scripture leads those summoned by it to the crucified Lord, as scripture it also becomes the judge of the institution visible as the Church which runs away from the Cross by promising the believer identity with itself through its own sacral power.

But even the Catholics of the present day cannot do other than ask themselves how Christians are to reach the truth of the community and thus the social identity of their faith without the institutionally guaranteed truth of scripture. And they cannot do other than ask themselves how Protestants intend to become a representative presence in post-Christian society without the protection of the publicly visible institution. In this, however, they betray the difficulties they are landed in by their own search for identity. And for this reason we must probe more deeply the significance for modern man's search for his or her identity of the awareness of scripture that had its origin in the Reformation.

In the complex confusion of the demands made on them by institutions and roles the citizens of the industrial nations are today asking again what the sources are of the totality of their threatened subjectivity. They feel the continuity of their history and their personal being threatened in the increasingly rapid change of social institutions and in the collapse of the traditions that sustained these. The oppressed who see themselves driven to destitution by the industrial nations must indeed look for the power with which they can identify themselves in the necessary struggle for liberation. Because in the situation they were in before the modern period the Reformers saw man's desperate plight not in his or her failure in himself or herself but in the power of his or her self-assurance, for this reason the effect of their prophetic reminder of scripture alone and of God's mercy alone is not linked to the modern age or that immediately preceding it or indeed to any particular age at all: it is only in invisible faith that man loses his or her obviously false life while true life is promised him or her. Hence I want to start with the Reformers' perception of scripture and to try to understand this as the place of that living voice that summons the individual and the Church today out of their despair over themselves to the identity of their selflessness: to the life that grows out of community with God's mercy, faithfulness and justice.

2. THE CATHOLIC LUTHER DISCOVERS THE BIBLE

At least until the 36th year of his life Luther was from every point of view an exemplary Catholic. Duly baptised, brought up in the school of the Brothers of the Common Life and in a parish school, after his basic studies (and once again influenced by Catholic popular piety) he entered the religious life, where he became a priest and teacher of theology. There was only one incurable disease he suffered from: the desire to become identical with Catholic piety and with the Church as a sacramental institution—and this went on at least until the attempt of 1512 to attain 'complete identity and agreement with God' through the mystical way of union.[3] His effort at continual confession and fasting can be evaluated as compulsive adaptation to the norms laid down by the institution but can also be seen as ethically a powerful achievement. It corresponded to the Church's teaching of the merit that the person moved by grace had to acquire for himself or herself and for others in order to become suitable for God's love. From a social and psychological point of view the image of this mature Catholic only displays neurotic traits for those who measure the inner logic of the Church's life by the categories of modern processes of socialisation.[4] If instead of psychoanalysing Luther's behaviour we judge it according to the demands of Catholic identity at the beginning of the sixteenth century, then we must talk of a socialisation that was completely successful in terms of the Church's life. The persistent temptation to see oneself as a sinner and a failure in the eyes of God was part of the essence of this Catholic piety.

The barely visible split in the fabric of Luther's Catholic identity is first seen by looking back at the effects of his work as a Reformer. In my view it is to be found in his virtually seismographical sensitivity to the Bible or, to put it in its own terms, in the event of his being addressed by the God who speaks through the biblical witness. However secondary and limited its interpretation may be in the context of the history of theology of that time, for Martin Luther it is God's own Word which according to the witness of scripture takes him captive and in this captivity liberates him. It will always remain impossible to decide whether it was the context of Luther's ecclesiastical and theological situation (late nominalism, the *devotio moderna*, the impetus of humanism) or the text of the Bible itself (especially through the Pauline epistles and the psalms) that in the framework of his life taught him to see the truth of scripture afresh. Every new experience emerges from the combined effect of someone who does the interpreting and the reality that is interpreted. However little we may know about the beginnings of Luther's reading of the Bible, three elements are prominent in his encounter with scripture.

First of all it is striking that it was not the proclamation of the Gospel, nor according to his statement prayer in common in choir, that opened up scripture to him. Rather common prayer brought him to the fear of alienation and thus to the state of doubt from which he sought to use individual verses from the Bible in continuous meditation. His interpretation is due essentially to this 'rumination' (Ps. 1:2), this 'choking in the Bible',[5] this inner life in scripture itself, and thus to continual meditation, testing and prayer in grappling with the reading of the text.

Secondly Luther from the start did not favour any theology that did not argue on the basis of biblical categories and biblical material. For this reason his first obligations to teach philosophy (1508–1509) and 'rancid' scholasticism (1509–1510) were, like scholastic studies, a burden that gave him no pleasure. He only found his true métier when in 1512 Staupitz put him into the chair of scripture. Now he entered into the service of the cause that overwhelmed him. If there is an event that provides the foundation of the Reformation long before its historical realisation and that does not cease up to the present day to unsettle the Catholic Church's identity, it is the event of being claimed completely by God's Word as witnessed in the Bible—and this precisely in the theological responsibility of the Church's teaching. Luther became the 'servant of Jesus Christ ... set apart for the gospel of God' (Rom. 1:1). But he did not become so like Paul as one 'called to be an apostle' but as one called to be a doctor of theology. Nothing is more characteristic of his style of teaching theology than the foreword to his first commentary on the psalms. It lets Jesus Christ himself speak: 'The foreword of Jesus Christ ... to the psalter of David. I am the door: if any one enters by me, he will be saved ... and find pasture (John 10:9)'.[6] Because for Luther what matters is the listening interpretation of the word that God speaks in scripture he began—and this was in contrast to the 'real' Reformation that was not planned in any way—by deliberately reforming the Wittenberg faculty of theology: it was turned into an academy of biblical exegesis. This faculty on which he set his mark became the mould for the institutions that the Reformation brought to realisation: Zwingli's *Prophezei* or biblical school in Zürich, Bullinger's scripture community at the monastery of Kappel, Bucer's exegetical lectures that preceded the founding of the university at Strasbourg, and also Calvin's lectureship at Geneva from which the Geneva Academy emerged in 1559. For thirty-three years Luther devoted himself to exegetical lectures, and of those twenty-five were on the Old Testament: 'By means of such teaching the papacy collapsed as far as I was concerned.'[7]

Thirdly Luther's, like Calvin's, understanding of scripture was based on the clear recognition of his own lack of understanding with regard to God's Word, though in itself God's Word was clear. The more the factual truth of the text revealed itself to the understanding the more it ran ahead of this understanding: progress in interpretation lay in recognising one's blindness with regard to the Word of God that was revealing itself clearly in this text. It was precisely this point that focused his objections both to enthusiasts and to Catholics: that they thought they knew scripture. 'Nothing is more harmful than when one mistakes and deceives onself that one believes and understands the gospel well.'[8] The enthusiasts were fighting on the basis of political necessity and according to Luther's harsh judgment on the basis of their own certainty instead of on the basis of trusting in God's Word: the Catholics on the other hand were using the wealth of their doctrine to build a wall against the voice of the living God. Even on the day before his death Luther bowed to the word of scripture that built up the community: 'Let no one think he has tasted enough of holy scripture already; for that he would have had to spend a hundred years with the prophets leading communities ... we are beggars. That is true.'

No one in the Catholic tradition had disputed that holy scripture possessed the highest authority in the Church. But according to the tradition the teaching authority was empowered by it to make the truth of scripture effectively valid as *norma normata* by means of definitions. But for Luther scripture was not merely the source but the clear water of truth itself. It became the book in which God himself addressed those who believed and validated their truth mediated through the preaching office. This broke the unity of Catholic identity: it came under the judgment of the proclamation of God's own Word.

3. THE CHIEF ARTICLE

When the sun rises then one can turn the light out. When it dawns on man how God acts justly towards him or her in the story of Jesus Christ the he or she can recognise the injustice even of his or her best efforts and can allow himself or herself to be led by this 'sun of justice'. As Luther put it as early as his first lecture on Rom. in 1515–1516: 'God wants to redeem us: not through the justice which from the start is our own, but through the justice and wisdom that comes to use from outside ... Hence it is essential for us to be instructed by this justice that really comes from outside and is quite alien to us. And so we must begin by casting out the justice that is originally our own.'[9]

In this happy exchange, as H. J. Iwand has called it, one can find the fundamental insight of the Reformation aleady expressed[10] if one merely distinguishes it from what it makes possible. The chief article of the Reformation on which depends everything 'that we teach and live against the pope, the devil and the world'[11] was not developed by Luther as the 'doctrine of justification'. The article of man's justification by faith alone does not intend to say anything other than the confession of the community whereby those who believe know they are completely accepted and reconciled by God's mercy in his Son's sacrifice of himself to the point of accepting death on the Cross. This confession excludes not only that man can justify himself or herself before God and his or her fellow men and women through his or her own action, but also that he or she can know anything at all about this desperate situation he or she is in and about his or her salvation from it apart from the gospel. In the gospel he or she is giving a binding promise of what no man can promise: his or her acceptance as a lost human being.

The chief article from which 'one cannot deviate or retreat at all, otherwise heaven and earth would fall', consists simply of a few biblical texts (Rom. 1:17, 3:21–28; John 1:29; Isa. 53:6). This could mislead Catholic readers into being tempted to interchange the Reformation perception of scripture with the modern biblicisim that uses biblical texts to help it work out a philosophy of life that is proof against all scientific knowledge and discovery. For Luther this kind of use of scripture is completely excluded. For Luther, in contrast to Thomas Aquinas, the statements of the Bible are not axioms of faith guaranteed by God's knowledge from which a human knowledge of faith can be deduced, but God's immediately topical utterances: they do what they say, and they say what they effect. They do not signify a reality independent of themselves but create the reality that already exists afresh. Because Martin Luther understands the Bible as 'God's witness of himself'[12] he has no problems in equating scripture with God's Word. Hence in it one must 'respect every jot and tittle more than the whole world, and before them we tremble and are afraid as before God himself'. Anyone therefore who does as scripture asks and 'says continually, teach me, teach me, teach me,'[13] is, as Luther graphically puts it, killed and raised up from the dead—in other words annihilated in his or her self-understanding and brought into a relationship of salvation with the God who is addressing him or her. As a hearer of the word man depends completely on the relationship which God grants or refuses him or her through his word witnessed in the Bible. It is *sola scriptura*, through the promise of the gospel, that the believer comes to his or her salvation *sola gratia*, through God's merciful self-sacrifice on the Cross. It is this and nothing else that is meant by the Reformation slogan *sola fide*, living by God's word.

4. SCRIPTURE: THE FOOLISHNESS OF GOD

If the Bible is to be perceived as the expression of God's action in utterance two elementary difficulties arise both for the Catholic tradition of the sixteenth century and for the historico-critical understanding of the Bible. From one point of view the text seems in this case to be theologically violated in its historical sense; from the other the question arises how a text should be able to be perceived in a binding fashion as the expression of God's own voice through our human manner of perception, given that man's sin makes him or her blind to God's truth. For Martin Luther this basic problem was less a problem to be tackled theoretically than rather the mystery of the Bible which only revealed itself in the performance of its exposition. As an interpreter of the Bible it was with increasing clarity that he described this mystery, which reveals to man the failure of his or her self-understanding and leads him or her to the identity of faith.

In his first approach Luther, from his first commentary on the psalms onwards, freed himself from the traditional division between the historical and the allegorical sense—allegorical including ecclesiastical, ethical and eschatological.[14] He grasped the difference more deeply, because he began to understand the contrast of 2 Cor. 3:6 ('The letter killeth, but the spirit giveth life') in the way that its two parts actively belong together. It is only God's spirit that decides whether the text as grasped by man leads to the fatal rejection of what it means or instead to the liberating recognition of its meaning. According to Luther's early theology of humility scripture is made use of by God himself in order to convict man of sin and thereby move him or her to accept his or her nothingness before God: in this way he or she reaches life from God's justice. Although for man's part everything depends on expounding the text in its literal sense with all the means that philology can provide, it can only be recognised by him or her as God's word if God gives man in his or her heart the Spirit of his word witnessed through scripture. For the Spirit who kills man's self that is concerned for itself alone in order to bring this self to life from God's Word can only be the Spirit through which God has spoken his Word. Hence Luther was opposed both to the charismatic independence with regard to the text shown by the enthusiasts and to the Spirit harnessed by the Catholic teaching authority and allowed to provide ecclesiastical authentication or even to judge the truth of God's Word. In this way the freedom of a Christian was brought into the Babylonian captivity of the Church. Obedience to God's Word on the other hand defined the existence of the Church as a selfless and therefore truly free existence.

Later Martin Luther defined the mystery of scripture, which since 1519 was governed by the key terms 'law' and 'gospel', entirely on the basis of its content. The single event towards which according to the New Testament all biblical evidence tends he now recognised (exclusively) in God's revelation of himself on the Cross and in the raising up of him who was crucified: in that the entire gospel was contained. 'Gospel' thus became a definition of content on the basis of which the sense not only of the New but also of the Old Testament was revealed. The counter-concept to 'gospel' is therefore not 'the Old Testament' but 'law', the entire curse of which Jesus Christ had taken on himself on the Cross (Gal. 3:13). But the effect of both the Old *and* the New Testament is the death-bringing effect of law when they are perceived independently of the gospel, that is, independently of God's action as it has been made manifest in the story of Jesus Christ. Isolated from the gospel the Bible burdens man through its demands as no other text does: it declares all guilty and robs all of the hope of a successful life. But in the light of the gospel the effect of the Old Testament is that of promise and of the New redemption. When as gospel the New Testament declares just the man who through the law has become a sinner before God and man it makes him or her just too. It gives him or her the Spirit of Christ and with that 'a happy and free heart, as the law demands'. The gospel enables man to do what he or she should do according to the law.

With this we have reached what is really meant by 'scripture'. It is the text that has the form of the Cross, the form of 'the foolishness of God'. In it God reveals his hiddenness and conceals his revelation. Just as through the Spirit the crucified one is recognised as the face of God 'who takes our weakness to himself' (Rom. 8:26), so the text of scripture testifies to God's voice through the Spirit of his Word: 'Since we have the same spirit of faith as is testified by the word of scripture ..., we too believe' (2 Cor. 4:13 from the German).

However much the Reformation split with the Roman Church may have been historically conditioned in its presuppositions, in the way it was carried out and in its consequences, it is only to a limited extent that it can be understood on the basis of these limiting conditions. The theologically based breach with the social identity of the Roman hierarchy, the practical revision of rite, sacramental practice and piety, and not least the new attitude towards the 'world' gained by Protestants cannot be explained merely historically: Protestant 'disobedience' towards the papal teaching authority has its basis and justification in the newly acquired obedience to God's own word. If something exists like a 'Reformation identity', then it consists of the unconditional recognition of God's Word that through scripture creates communities and in these addresses individuals to guide and redeem them. Through the recognition of the 'foolishness of God' which became manifest in the crucifixion of Jesus Christ and which has 'made foolish the wisdom of the world' (1 Cor. 1:20) Protestants shattered not only their identity with the power and wisdom of the Roman Catholic Church but, seen at a profounder level, also their identity as men and women who could justify themselves.

5. 'AS IT WAS WRITTEN'

What was and is decisive for Israel is the fact that, speaking symbolically, God himself wrote the two tablets of the law (cf. Exod. 24:12, 31:18, and elsewhere). The text turned to stone symbolises God's faithfulness: in what is written on the first tablet God turns to his people to free them—'I am the Lord your God, who brought you out of the land of Egypt, out of the house of bondage' (Exod. 20:2, Deut. 5:6)—and then on the second tablet burns the law of freedom into the heart of those he has freed. By means of this claim to promise and direct God makes history with his people through a text. And for this reason the point of the history of Israel is to tell 'what has been written'. What is written makes it possible to be addressed by the event that with its promise provides the foundation and justification for Israel's present: 'In every generation a man is obliged to regard himself in such a way as if *he* had come out of Egypt.'[15] If the texts of the prophets written down before the Exile already emerged critically as a 'third source of authority' alongside the institution of royal power and the sacrificial worship of the priests, then the Deuteronomistic reformation was right to base Judaism on the Word alone. What Yahweh proclaimed to Moses on Mount Horeb now provides the foundation and justification for the continuity of the people of God that shapes their identity: 'Gather the people to me, that I may let them hear my words, so that they may learn to fear me all the days that they live upon the earth, and that they may teach their children so' (Deut. 4:10, cf. 5:1, 6:7,20; Exod. 13:8; and elsewhere). Remembering, handing on and retelling afresh what the God of Israel does when he speaks to his people compelled after the Exile the formation of the corresponding social institution, the synagogue. Its shrine is the roll of the Torah, the 'book of instruction'.[16] It becomes the primary image of the community that lives from the proclamation of 'holy scripture'.

As a Jew who was concerned precisely about this identity of his people, Jesus asked the Sadducees on the decisive question of the resurrection: 'Is not this why you are wrong, that you know neither the scriptures nor the power of God? ... Have you not read in the book of Moses, in the passage about the bush, how God said to him, "I am the God of Abraham, and the God of Isaac, and the God of Jacob"? He is not God of the dead, but of the living' (Mark 12:24–27). By 'knowing' scriptures and the power of God (that is, his Spirit) God shows himself as the living one who wakes the dead. After Jesus had opened the scriptures himself in this power to the women who were following him and to the men he had called (Matt. 7:29 and Jn. 3:34), the community was able to understand and proclaim even his death and resurrection 'according to scripture'. He had indeed truly fulfilled both tablets of the law: according to the promise (Acts 13:32) he 'rose again on the third day according to scripture'; but according to the law that guides and instructs he 'dies for our sins in accordance with the scriptures' (1 Cor. 15:3).

Martin Luther was right to draw attention to the fact that for the Christian community 'scripture' (historically and as a matter of principle) means the Old Testament. This scripture attains its goal in the revelation of the history of Jesus Christ, which is nothing but God's promise and living voice and hence something that deserves to be yelled abroad.[17] For Christ fulfilled the Old Testament as law (by living up to what it demanded) and at the same time brought it to an end (by letting himself be cursed by it on the Cross). By his death and resurrection he brought the promise of the old covenant for the first time fully into force: his story is the promise of God himself, God's living Word, which mercifully raises up those judged by the law and brings them to life. The fact that this word was once again written down as the 'New Testament' was regarded by Luther as a 'great loss and lack of spirit'[18] because the gospel that creates the communities of the new covenant is 'written not with ink but with the Spirit of the living God, not on tablets of stone but on tablets of human hearts' (2 Cor. 3:3, cf. Ezek. 11:19, Jer. 31:31–34). The gospel can and must therefore be proclaimed.

The Christian community finds its way to its identity by remembering what the scripture of the Old Testament reveals in promise and guidance. But it is only through the fulfilment of this scripture that it becomes the people of God: through the crucified one who has been raised up and who sends his Spirit into its heart. For this reason the Christian Church is no 'religion of the book' but is rather the people summoned by the voice of God, that is, by Jesus Christ, the people that has to proclaim to the entire world the fulfilment of scripture. This is the good contradiction that the Christian community has to oppose to the modern 'industrialisation of historical thinking' (Arnold Toynbee) and thus to the loss of continuity.

6. THE IDENTITY OF SELFLESSNESS

The powerful institutions of the modern age—the nation, industry, and the media—make such a claim on everyone who comes into this world that he or she can only be afraid for his or her self. The search for strengthening one's ego and self-affirmation, for distancing oneself from one's role and for wholeness has its basis in the need for the individual to ensure his or her freedom within the actual lack of freedom of his or her history.[19] But the dilemma of freedom does not leave the individual any choice: he or she can only realise himself or herself either by 'playing' the roles provided or by opposing them by virtue of his or her isolation. In the first case he or she despairs of himself or herself by affirming the whole that is provided as his or her own life (whether this whole is 'the depth of the self' or the 'progress' of the economy, technology and science with the sacrifice it demands or simply the 'progress of freedom'). In the second case this whole becomes for the individual something absurd that he or she still affirms while rejecting it (even suicide is an affirmation of the life for whose sake it is being thrown away).

Scripture summons its hearers neither along the path of the isolated self nor into Church 'roles' that still have to be played alongside all the others. Rather as law it exposes precisely the despair that lies in the fact that we have to realise our lives ourselves without really being able to do so. The judgment of God's justice pronounces us guilty by making manifest the actual injustice of our love, our hopes and the action of our faith. And in this way scripture shatters the pretence of our social and subjective identity and the illusion of a 'succesful life'. The law 'kills' our alleged self, it 'makes' us sinners.

As gospel the entire scripture proclaims only one single event: God's love which accepts human beings in their injustice as they are. By becoming man God enters into solidarity with those who realise themselves in vain. By his sacrifice of himself on the Cross he shows the unconditional nature of his love even towards those who self-confidently condemn him. The gospel is the event of the recognition of sinners and judgment on sin. It thereby frees people from their selves that are in fact blinded and puts them into a relationship with God. The gospel accepts into God's own humanity man who cannot himself or herself do justice to himself or herself. By this it makes those summoned by it selfless. In this selflessness people can do justice to their fellow men and women: they find their identity in the selflessness expected of them. Because they know they are accepted as guilty before God and their fellow men and women they become capable of accepting themselves and recognising in the face of others the justice they have injured: they become capable of forming a community. The gospel expounded by the Reformation does not only expose the guilt of the Churches that do not do justice to each other. Rather it summons them together to the battle against sin, from whose violence the oppressed are fatally suffering and in whose power the oppressors cannot find their way to their brothers and sisters.

Translated by Robert Nowell

Notes

1. Martin Luther *Dictata super psalterium*, in Martin Luther *Studienausgabe*, edited by H. U. Delius, vol. 1 (East Berlin 1979) p. 40; WA (Weimarer Ausgabe) 3:25.
2. On Luther's attitude to scholasticism cf. especially O. H. Pesch *Theologie der Rechtfertigung bei Martin Luther und Thomas von Aquin. Versuch eines systematisch-theologischen Dialogs* (Mainz ²1985 with bibliograph), and his *Hinführung zu Luther* (Mainz 1982).
3. Cf. the convincing biography by M. Brecht *Martin Luther. Sein Weg zur Reformation 1483–1521* p. 101.
4. Thus E. H. Erikson *Der junge Mann Luther. Eine psychoanalytische und historische Studie* (Frankfurt-am-Main 1975) especially pp. 187–245.
5. TR 1:320 no. 674, 4:432, 20 no. 4691; on what follows cf. WA 50:695.
6. *Dictata* ed. cit. p. 33; WA 3:12.
7. WA 30:III:386; cf. D. Schellong *Calvins Auslegung der synoptischen Evangelien* (Munich 1969) pp. 9–13; O. H. Pesch *Hinführung* (note 2 above) pp. 48–70.
8. TR 1:414, 15 no. 849, 6:114, 29 no. 6680; the quotation that follows is from TR 5:317, 16 no. 5677.
9. Martin Luther *Vorlesung über den Römerbreif* in *Studienausgabe* (note 1 above) p. 100; WA 56:158.

10. Cf. H. J. Iwand *Luthers Theologie, Nachgelassene Werke*, vol. 15 (Munich 1974) p. 45. For the ever-continuing debate on the Reformation break cf. B. Lohse (ed.), *Der Durchbruch der reformatorischen Erkenntnis bei Luther* (Darmstadt 1968).

11. On this and what follows cf. the Schmalkaldic Articles of 1537 in *Die Bekenntnisschriften der evangelisch-lutherischen Kirche* (Göttingen 1982) pp. 405–468, in this case pp. 416–417; cf. also O. H. Pesch *Hinführung* (note 2 above) pp. 264–271.

12. WA 50:282; the quotation that follows WA 26:450. For the whole cf. P. Schempp *Theologische Entwürfe* (Munich 1973) pp. 10–74.

13. TR 4:616, 36 no. 5017.

14. Cf. G. Ebeling *Lutherstudien*, vol. 1 (Tübingen 1971) pp. 1–68.

15. Mishnah, Pes. X:5 with reference to Ex. 13:8. Cf. also Romans 4:23–24, 1 Cor. 9:10, etc. Cf. J. Ebach 'Verstehen, Lernen und Erinnerung in der hebräischen Bibel' in *Der evangelische Erzieher* 38 (1986) pp. 106–155. For what follows cf. A. Lemaire *Le écoles et la formation de la Bible dans l'ancien Israel* (Fribourg/Göttingen 1981).

16. Cf. R. Riesner *Jesus als Lehrer. Eine Untersuchung zum Ursprung der Evangelien-Überlieferung* (Tübingen ²1984) pp. 123–153, and for what follows pp. 246–502.

17. WA 6:2.

18. WA 10:I:1:627.

19. On this dialectic which breaks into German idealism from within cf. T. Pröpper *Erlösungsglaube und Freiheitsgeschichte. Eine Skizze zur Theologie* (Munich 1985); a more idealistic and psychological treatment is provided by J. Werbick *Glaube im Kontext. Prolegomena zu einer elementaren Theologie* (Zürich/Einsiedeln/Cologne 1983).

Isabelle Chareire

The Part Played by Christ and the Spirit in the Identification Process

OTHER ARTICLES in this issue are devoted to looking at Christianity from the outside: to defining it by its differences from other world views. From unbelief first, through its recognition of a dimension that transcends human beings; from the 'natural religion' dear to the eighteenth century, in that it is a revealed religion (a reference to a God who speaks, a God who happens in history); finally, in regard to the great monotheisms, Christianity recognises a one and triune God, Father, Son and Spirit. It is here that we should look for the unique marks of Christianity if we are to understand it within its own dynamic.

Identifying, in effect, means distinguishing an object (person or thing) by referring it to a particular determinant, external or internal. Identify (from *idem*, same) is proclaimed in relation to an otherness and, at the same time, in an inner dynamic proper to the object. Taking away the first stage leaves an object closed in on itself, in-determinate, blurred; removing the second leaves the subject without real consistency, dispersed into its multiple determinants but without its inner 'spring', vitality. The identity of a being lies within this dialectic between the self and the world.

The term 'identification' is equivocal. The transitive form of the verb *to identify* has a cognitive meaning: to identify someone is to recognise him; but psychologists use it with a reflexive pronoun: to identify with. We shall use it in this second sense here to see how the relationship of subject to model is worked out in identification processes as understood by psychoanalysis.

94 THE PART PLAYED BY CHRIST AND THE SPIRIT

1. THE IDENTIFICATION PROCESS AND CHRISTIAN IDENTITY

(a) The identification process

J. Lacan defines identification as 'the transformation produced in a subject through adopting an image'.[1] In the process of give and take between the self and the world the personality of every being is developed, evolves, by reference to models, certain aspects of which it assimilates, only to reject later in order to take on others. A child's first models are generally its parents; others come later. For a believer, the key-reference is to the founder of the religion.

Psychologists usually distinguish four stages in the child's identification process.[2] On discovering its separation from its mother, the child of under three will seek to protect itself from the world through the mediation of either father or mother. The anxiety produced by its new autonomy leads the child to project an idealised image on this adult, who becomes an ideal model in which the child seeks its own idealised image in its wish to conform to what the other expects of it, since it dreads losing this other. The other is therefore not seen in its otherness, but distorted by the narcissistic projections in which the child looks for itself. This identification is called 'imaginary' because within a dual relationship it is seeking, in the other, an ideal self which cannot exist.

In the next stage, which is also that of the Oedipus ordeal, the child comes up against the ban placed by the father on its desire for an exclusive relationship with its mother. Its relationship to the other is mediatised by—to use Lacan's well-known play on words, *l'interdit exprimé par le langage*—(through) *inter-dict*, expressed in language. By appearing to oppose the child's wish, the father is seen as all-powerful, and therefore non-wanting, because complete in himself. As long as the child holds to this ideal perception of its father, who 'inter-dicts' its wish it cannot move beyond the narcissistic image it has of itself. It needs to discover that its father is limited, mortal, in order to come to terms with its wish and so accept itself as a finite subject.[3] This stage is called 'structuring' or 'symbolic' since it is the stage of mediation.

Imaginary identification (the narcissistic confirmation necessary because it allows the subject to accept itself as a unity) is immediate: it is what happens when one discovers one's image in a mirror.[4] In symbolic identification, on the other hand, the child discovers itself in 'the time of death and history':[5] language shows it the radical otherness of the world, and the total failure of any object to meet its wish for it. Psychoanalysts symbolise this ever-unsatisfied wish by the phallus, the fourth element introduced into the Oedipus triangle to denote the inaccessible 'which no object equals but of which every object is made up'.[6] While the narcissistic stage tends to close the subject in on itself in the quest for an inaccessible idealised image of itself,

Narcissus in his pool, the symbolic stage, the ordeal of reality and one's definitive incompleteness, teaches the child to manage its wish before the world.

(b) Christianity as an existential adventure

If revelation is 'the coming of a truth' rather than of 'a knowledge',[7] then Christianity is an existential adventure in which this identification process through reference needs to be analysed. The reference here is Jesus Christ, who offers salvation and life by inviting us to follow him: see Luke 6:47; 14:25–33, etc. What does following Jesus mean? Does it mean imitating him?[8]

Being a Christian means above all placing one's trust in a historical personage in whom we accept a trans-historical dimension. It means identifying Jesus of Nazareth with the Messiah announced by the Prophets and expected by the Jewish people. This recognition comes through our experience of the risen Christ: an event handed down by tradition through the Christian community, and a personal adventure at the same time. While the act of faith has a content (its *creditum*), our *credo*, our act of faith itself, the movement of trust that impels us toward the object in which we believe, is just as important. The way we make this act of faith is just as characteristic of Christian faith as its content, which needs to be assimilated in a certain way. This new way of living our relationship with God is inherent in the revelation of a trinitarian God: this revelation was given to us by Jesus Christ and continues to be breathed into us by the Spirit. If this God who relates to us offers us, in God's mode of being, a model on which to form our personality as believers, then we also need to understand how the relationship between Father, Son and Spirit works, and to analyse the consequences for us.

2. THE PLACE OF CHRIST IN CHRISTIAN FAITH

(a) Jesus of Nazareth

Christian faith is rooted in an event that took place both within and outside history. In Jesus of Nazareth, God took flesh of our flesh (John 1:1–18; Matt. 1 and 2; Luke 1 and 2), and revealed his glory in this *in-carnation*, this manifestation of God in the man Jesus.

Jesus came at a time of messianic expectation among the Jewish people.[9] In his actions and words he proclaimed the kingdom of God, in which all who hunger in body and spirit will be satisfied. But he did not underpin the strict piety of the orthodox Jews; on the contrary, he challenged it. He did not take part in political movements (Matt. 22:17–22) and so did not aim to restore the earthly kingdom of the people of Yahweh. While afraid of conversing with no one, he nevertheless chose to address himself to those pushed out to the margins of society. He spoke to women with a bad reputation (Luke 7:37–50), shared meals with publicans and sinners (Matt. 9:10–11), showed forgiveness to people punished by the Law or shunned by the righteous: Zaccheus, the woman of Samaria, the woman taken in adultery; yet he was just as ready to talk at night to the Pharisee Nicodemus (Luke 19:1–10, John 4:6–16; 8:3–11; 3:1–21).

After his Galilean Spring, his preaching suffered rejection (Mark 7, etc.), but despite this, he remained true to his word and the way he had chosen to proclaim it (Luke 4:1–13, etc.). This determination led him to his passion and death on the Cross. Faced with this apparent setback, we have to ask two questions: what is the relationship between Jesus of Nazareth and the experience of the risen Christ which lies at the heart of all Christian experience? And, what is the connection between the Jesus of history and the Christ of faith? And another: what is the meaning of this resurrection which apparently left the course of history untouched, leading some exegetes to speak of *delaying* the Parousia?

(*b*) Differentiated unity

Over the past fifty years, several analyses of this complicated relationship between Jesus and the Christ have appeared. In his *Messianisme de Jésus et discretion de Dieu*,[10] Christian Duquoc seeks a way of overcoming the opposition between the interpretation deriving from Bultmann on the one hand, and his opponents on the other, an opposition he sees starting with Jacques Pohier's *Quand je dis Dieu*.[11]

Under the influence of recent historical discoveries, Bultmann, writing in the 1930s, downgraded the Jesus of history, stating that we can only know him in the transforming light of the Christ of the kerygma, and that in any case only this Christ matters to our faith. So Jesus of Nazareth, in all the density of his individual, limited, existence is submerged by the splendour of the resurrection, existing only in the shadow of Christ. This link between the two aspects of the personality of Jesus is known as 'kerygmatic unity' since it brings them together under the predominance of the risen Christ proclaimed by the kerygma.

Pohier challenged this diminution of the contingent dimension of Jesus, seeing the general interpretation of both redemption and resurrection as producing a similar diminution, based on a rejection of our human condition. Seeing redemption in this way would remove us from our condition and assimilate us to the divine; this is no more than the old sin of Adam and Eve:

wanting to be like God. And such a belief in the resurrection would hide a refusal of death, a make-believe wish-fulfilment seeing itself capable of escaping from negativity in the unboundedness of its own fulfilment. Pohier claimed that stress should rather be laid on the contingent and practical nature of Jesus' preaching.

Duquoc proposes to conceive the unity between Jesus of Nazarth and the risen Christ in differentiated form: 'the kerygma lives from the narrative and the narrative is opened to universality by the kerygma';[12] to take one without the other produces either a gnosis or illusion of the will, or an anecdote with no theological value. In order to apprehend this unity, he puts forward three lines of thought: discovering anticipatory signs of the resurrection in the life of the Nazarene; maintaining the endurance of reality in its negative aspects— contingency and death; 'separating paschal faith from illusory wish'.

Jesus' life shows us that God's first concern is to promote the wellbeing of those threatened by oppression, exclusion and every attack on the integrity of their person. In this task, Jesus showed complete trust in his Father, a trust that set him free in the face of the risks his actions involved. Duquoc sees this freedom in action and word as the anticipatory sign of the paschal event at the very heart of Jesus' earthly life.

Giving one's life, however, can be a form of denying death: fearlessness in the face of death can be a way of not facing up to its reality. Duquoc resolves this quandary by stressing that Jesus' action is based on his trust in the promise of Yahweh, and that, furthermore, it is not natural death that is challenged here, but violent death, unjustifiable oppression. The contradictory nature of this double experience of Jesus' faith, hope in the promise coupled with realisation of the endless renewal of violence, is expressed in Jesus' agonised cry from the cross: 'My God, my God, why have you forsaken me?' (Mark 15:34). His calling on the Father from the very heart of his despair shows the tension between the strength of hope and the cruelty of reality. Faced with his aggressors, Jesus does not become part of the cycle of violence:[13] he does not meet violence with violence, as the power of the world would, nor with sanctions, as the law would, because violence bears its destructive power within itself, and he is its first victim. Seen in this way, Easter does not mean the abolition of the limits of human existence, but proclaims that 'murder has no future, and death is overcome because murder has no future'.[14] 'He who would save his life must lose it': it is only in letting go of an object that one attains it.

The originality of this 'differentiated unity' is also to be found in its distinction between the historical and the contingent. If the history of society is human history, not natural history, this is because human beings manage their relationship to the contingent in a historical fashion. This means that historical action, contingent in itself, sets itself the task of resisting human precariousness, through setting up institutions and developing culture. So differentiated unity would not set the paschal faith in the contingency of Jesus of Nazareth, which would mean denying his existence in its negativity, but in the historical dimension of his actions and his words. So paschal faith does not spring from the (imaginary and natural) desire to abolish limitation, but arises as a possibility of changing natural human relationships into historical relationships (in the positive sense of 'historical' described above).

(c) Jesus' messianism

This differentiated unity keeps the paradox of Jesus being true God and true man; it genuinely upholds both sides, giving them their full value, without submerging one in the other. This enables us to grasp the ambiguous nature of Christian messianism. In practice, whether we look at Jesus' messianism before or after the experience of the resurrection, it is unsatisfying from the Jewish standpoint which Jesus claimed to inherit. His messianism is carried out 'in liberating obedience, not in proclaiming the all-powerfulness of God'.[15] Jesus died because of his message; the 'already there' aspect of the kingdom he proclaimed was set back by his adversaries. Through the resurrection, God authenticated his action, and reiterated his promise;[16] this promise, however, is not obviously fulfilled in history: violence continues. So we can speak of the parousia being delayed, of some sort of failure in the history of salvation! Or perhaps we have to view the resurrection event in its prolongation in the ascension and pentecost in order to understand this delay in grace.

3. THE SPIRIT OF DIFFERENCE

The coming of the Spirit has often been seen as an outpouring of God's almighty power. R. Sublon, re-reading pneumatology in the light of psychoanalysis,[17] suggests that it should instead be seen as the production of difference, and so as the creation of identity. Writing as theologian and psychoanalyst, he begins by stressing the extent to which the Jewish people's experience of liberation is an experience of renouncing divine immediacy. We cannot see God face-to-face without dying; we meet God only in the barely perceptible, as Moses and Elijah found (Exod. 33:18–23; 1 Kings 19:11–13). This constantly renewed passage from idolatry, meaning contemplating oneself in an idealised image, to true piety, leads to believers accepting the difference between themselves and the Creator. This difference enables them to place themselves in relation to a God whose presence is shown as absence. This experience leads to the hidden God in Jesus Christ, and to the coming of the Spirit.

(a) The Oedipean impasse of the Holy Family

Sublon goes on to say that if one looks at the structure of the Holy Family alone, one is faced with an impasse of the Oedipus conflict. So Jesus was born not of the will of a mother and father with no more than a juridical bond between them; he was a gift from heaven, 'arriving after the previous renunciation of desire by both halves of the couple'.[18] Behind this Oedipean triangle, in which there is no wish that has to be dealt with, and where therefore each of the persons cannot be distinguished from the others, looms the shadow of an ideal, castrating father. Fixed in this closed world, Jesus would fuse his identity into this image of the all-powerful father. His death would then represent the murder or castration of the father, and his resurrection the restoration of the image of the ideal father, an image in which believers can contemplate themselves like Narcissus in his pool.

The doctrine of the Trinity, on the other hand, at least in its Latin form,[19] can be understood as the way out of this narcissistic impasse.

(b) From sign to signifier

The Oedipus conflict is resolved through the advent of a possibility. The possible, situated between what is not and what is absolutely, opens up an avenue of freedom in the realm of 'can be'. Speech is a manifestation of this area of possibility.

Speech is not innate; learning to speak is learning to dip into a common fund that already exists: this common fund will therefore not always express 'my' particularity. There is something inexpressible in wish, in the singularity of the I expressing it, an inexpressibility stemming not from an ineffable metaphysic, but from the structure of language. There is an imbalance between my wish as I experience it and my wish as I express it: an alienation of subject from language that there is no way round. No way round, because speech alone enables me to become conscious of myself, while in my speech I emerge as another, different from what I confusedly feel myself to me before expressing myself in speech.

The world is not the object: this impossibility of making a complete identification between signifier and signified forces me to renounce immediate and complete satisfaction of my wish. To indicate my wish, I address words to another—who provokes both my use of speech and my consciousness of myself—and signifiers that date from before me. So I distinguish myself from the rest of the world, mark out my difference and make 'the objects I name part of the symbolic universe'.[20] The signifier thus becomes a metaphor for me, representing me to others. But it can never be an adequate representation of me and my wishes, whose meaning it always referred further, from signifier to signifier. The essential function of the signifier is to distinguish one signified from other signifieds, to express its difference rather than give an abstract account of its content.

Sign, on the other hand, is this effort (or this illusion) to tell the content of the thing expressed. Lacan defines sign as representing something to someone who receives it. But the identity of one and the other remains in a state of flux; they are not defined or distinguished. To say that God is revealed through signs risks confusing God with human beings: who can interpret the sign, except its recipients, and will they not find signs where they wish to see them?

(c) The resurrection as metaphorical signifier

Furthermore, if we look at the Creator-creation relation from the standpoint of fatherhood and sonship, to say that Jesus is the sign of the Father can lead to confusion of one with the other. Now while the Gospels (basically John) use expressions such as 'the Father and I are one' (John 10:30), they also indicate the distance that separates Jesus from his Father; in the passion, clearly, but also in knowing 'that day and hour' (Matt. 24:36). So should we not think of revelation as being in the symbolic order, in the sense that Lacan uses the term, that is as signifying the distance between the Creator and his creation, and therefore introduce the Spirit into our reading of the resurrection?

Based on Jacques Delorme's exegesis,[21] Sublon points to the series of couplets of opposed terms that fill the proclamation of the Easter faith: death-life, humbling-raising up, ignominy-glory and so on. These oppositions cannot be resolved by fusing the two contradictory terms, nor by abandoning one in favour of the other. To do this would be to hold that the time of equivocacy has passed away, and, like gnostics and milleniarists, to say that perfect clarity has come with the eschaton. But since the resurrection has not produced this time of perfect light, the Spirit cannot be seen as the emanation of the all-powerfulness of God. Such an emanation would in any case be contrary to the movement of creation, since God creates by separating aeons, not by emanation from them.[22]

The resurrection should then not be interpreted as the Son going back to the Father and recovering his divine privileges, which are then, through the Spirit as intermediary, handed on to the believing community, but as a metaphorical signifier. In other words, a space open to the senses, an interval in which 'I', represented by the signifier, am defined by my difference. It is only the existence of this difference, this distance from others, that opens up the area of the possible. While 'sign' appears to be univocal, 'signifier' comes to be the mark of the difference between what it should mean and what it does mean, so open to different interpretative possibilities. The sign, Jesus, disappears to leave a signifier: a cave, the empty tomb.

(d) The Spirit creator of difference and sameness

From sign to signifier: this is the transition from Jesus to Nazareth to the risen Christ who brings about the coming of the Spirit. The language of the resurrection is both the emptiness of the tomb and the breath of the Spirit. Through Jesus, God is revealed to us as Father: resurrection-pentecost makes us sharers in this sonship, thereby establishing us in a difference, recognised and named, from our Creator.

The Spirit signifies the distance between Father and Son within the intra-trinitarian relationship, and through the economy of revelation. In the Latin translation of the Symbol of Constantinople,[23] the *Filioque* underlines the double procession of the Spirit from Father and Son: the fruit of its relationship to a reality that is at once two and one. Father and Son are a sole source,[24] and yet each exists by reason of his difference from the other. God, different in himself, escapes from narcissistic contemplation of himself. This distance is made manifest to us through the gift of the Spirit at pentecost: the non-fulfilment of the promise at easter signifies the distance existing between Jesus and God. At the same time, as Duquoc stresses, this coming of the Spirit, which opens up the promise but does not complete it, 'authenticates the form of messianism chosen by Jesus'.[25] Yahweh once more shows himself not in the noise of the storm but in the 'sound of a gentle breeze'.

CONCLUSION

Looking back over the elements we have taken from these authors—the differentiated unity between Jesus and the Christ, the resurrection as metaphorical signifier, and the Spirit signifying the separation between Jesus and his Father, what can we now say about the process of Christian identification?

The relationship of Jesus of Nazareth to the risen Christ in the differentiated mode invites us to a certain type of relationship with Jesus Christ. The act of faith appears where the sign disappears. After the disappearance of Jesus' body,[26] the relationship of Christians to Christ is no longer borne by the world of the senses, but is operated through the mediation of the Spirit, and it is at the heart of this mediation that we experience the resurrection. The empty tomb points to Jesus' irreducible contingency, the linen clothes lying on the ground (John 20:6–7), and Jesus' assumption of his earthly life with his Father, leaving the grave empty. Following Jesus means first accepting the contingency of his particular being-there, and recognising, in this being-there, the irreducibility of his otherness. But the disappearance of the sign in its sensory otherness does not simply lead to an imaginary identification. Identification with Christ is effectively mediated by his absence, signified by the Spirit. And this absence is the setting for the founding of Christian identity. Besides placing the Son in his difference from the Father, the Spirit establishes us in a true relationship with the Creator and with the Creator's manifestation in Christ. *Being in relationship with* means *defining oneself relative to*: placing—so distancing—born of otherness.

So following Jesus does not mean imitating him, in the sense of reproducing a given model, a prototype; such imitation stems from a relationship of fusion. Following Jesus means first taking up ourselves, in our double aspect of singularity and common contingency, so that, open to the Spirit who cries 'Abba' in us, we can be won over to that same freedom of action and word that allowed Jesus of Nazareth, as himself and as a man of his time, to denounce oppression and proclaim the coming of the kingdom. So the Spirit, through creative reading of the word, through reappropriating the word in the spirit of the Sermon on the Mount, opens the believing community to a symbolic type of identification with Christ.

The incarnation shows us the beauty of the world afresh, in its very finiteness; the redemption sets us free from the yoke of sin. Established as we are, thanks to the Spirit, in our difference from God, we have to pass over from the guilt which fossilises us by projecting an ideal of ourselves which we suffer ceaselessly through not being able to live up to, to the humility through which we accept ourselves as creatures of grace and freedom.

We have continually to tear ourselves up from the land of our birth, from the imaginary sweetness of a world without otherness and without constraints, so as to be, in the words of the poet Patrice de la Tour du Pin:[27]

> Those whom you take, Jesus, but those you make anew
> To be the child they bring to birth:
> Far from the old dream in which I dreamed
> Only of a garden, a haven
> Of peace, with its plants
> Happy through eternity.

You cut them down, Jesus, and destroy me with them,
But it is me myself you sow
And make the kernel of my fruit:
I have known you in your call
And it is you yourself
Who make me carry what I am.

Translated by Paul Burns

Notes

1. J. Lacan 'Le Stade du miroir comme formateur de la fonction du Je' in *Ecrits* 1 (1970) p. 90.
2. Leaving aside the primary and independent stages of identification, which are less important for our purpose here.
3. Cf. R. Sublon 'L'Esprit Saint dans la perspective psychanalytique' in *L'Esprit Saint* (Brussels 1978) pp. 97–130.
4. Lacan *op. cit.*
5. C. B. Clément 'Imaginaire, symbolique et réel' in *Encyclopédie Larousse* (1974) pp. 6120–6122.
6. M. Safouan, quoted in Sublon *op. cit.*
7. Sublon *op. cit.*
8. H. Linard de Guertechin 'Suivre Jésus est-ce l'imiter? Approche psychologique de l'identification au Christ' in *Rev. Théol. de Louvain* 15 (1984) pp. 5–27.
9. Cf. Ch. Perrot *Jésus et l'histoire* (Paris 1979).
10. Geneva 1984.
11. Paris 1978.
12. *Op. cit.* p. 81.
13. See the studies by R. Girard, particularly *Des choses cachées depuis la fondation du monde* (Paris 1978): 'Violence cannot tolerate the continued existence within its realm of a being who owes it nothing, who pays it no homage and forms the single possible threat to its rule. What it does not understand ... is that, in getting rid of Jesus by its usual means, it falls into the trap that only such an innocence could set for it, because it is ultimately not a trap: there is nothing hidden. It shows its own hand to the point of being for ever stricken in its basic operation; the more it seeks to hide its pitiful secret by making it work with all its might, the more it succeeds in revealing it' (p. 233).
14. Duquoc *op. cit.* p. 87.
15. B. Lauret 'Christologie dogmatique' in *Initiation à la Pratique de la Théologie* II (Paris 1982) p. 286.
16. Cf. Acts 1:7–8.
17. Sublon *op. cit.*
18. *Ibid.* p. 112.

19. In the Latin confession, the Spirit proceeds from the Father *and* the Son; in the Greek tradition, the Spirit proceeds from the Father through the Son, a less precise formulation which still leaves the *Filioque* possibility open.

20. Sublon *op. cit.* p. 117.

21. J. Delorme 'La Résurrection de Jésus dans le langage du Nouveau Testament' in *Le langage de la foi dans l'Ecriture et dans le monde actuel* (Paris 1972), quoted by Sublon *op. cit.* p. 120.

22. In gnostic vocabulary, aeons are eternal powers emanating from the Supreme Being, through which he works in the world.

23. DS 188.

24. Cf. St Augustine *De Trinitate* V,14,15: 'But just as the Father and the Son are one sole God, and, with regard to creation one sole creator and one sole Lord in a *relative* manner, so with regard to the Holy Spirit they are, in a *relative* manner, but one sole source' (my italics). ET *On the Trinity* in *Fathers of the Church* vol. 45 (Washington DC 1963).

25. Duquoc *op. cit.* p. 353.

26. On this subject see Hegel's comments on the conquest of the Holy Sepulchre by the Crusades, in *Leçons sur la philosophie de l'histoire* (Paris ³1970) pp. 301–306.

27. P. de la Tour du Pin *Concert Eucharistique* (Paris 1971) p. 63.

PART IV

Identity and Verification

Pierre de Locht

The Role and the Limits of Personal and Communal Ethical Practices in Establishing Christian Identity

OVER A long period Christians believed, and in some measure continue to believe, that they have a monopoly in moral values, or at least a clear superiority in the perception and practice of those values. Emerging from a 'Christian' world, we are at present engaged in discovering both a genuine rigorously-observed morality among non-Christians and agnostics, and plenty of gaps in the way of life of Christians, as well as in our Church's capacity to evaluate and support the moral development of humanity. Could it be, then, that this area, which seemed to be the prerogative of Christianity and which we thought gave us our identity, is not after all where our identity is to be found?

However, the message of Jesus does not only indicate a collection of beliefs; it also implies a new manner of living. The Gospels emphasise the close link between the love of God and the service of our brothers. 'By this love you have for one another, everyone will know that you are my disciples' (John 13:35). 'In the same way your light must shine in the sight of men, so that, seeing your good works, they may give the praise to your Father in heaven' (Matt. 5:16). It is therefore not only in ideas or beliefs that Christian identity is located and finds expression, but in the way people live. What sort of a faith would it be that was not incarnated in a way of life?

But in that case where can we locate the ethical identity peculiar to Christianity?

THE LIMITS OF PERSONAL AND COMMUNAL ETHICS

1. THE CONSEQUENCES OF LINKING CHRISTIAN IDENTITY TO DULY CODIFIED MORAL BEHAVIOUR

1. Insofar as certain clearly-defined ethical options are the specific location of our identity, it becomes difficult, if not impossible, to *recognise in others somewhat similar moral values*. Unless we can 'take over' these morally exemplary non-Christians by recognising them as 'Christians without knowing it', how can we give proper recognition to their way of life without calling into question what we claim as our own (exclusive) characteristics?

So long as we lived in a protected, unanimous universe, we could ignore the way of life of agnostics. Happily such blindness is less easily achieved today in the perpetual ferment brought about by our modern life. Nevertheless some people still try to recreate this body of 'right-thinkers', by ignoring or caricaturing opposing positions, if only to avoid having to come to terms with what is 'different'.

2. If certain clearly-defined forms of behaviour constitute our identity, they become *untouchable*. Nothing is negotiable, nothing can be re-examined in the light of new developments—for example in the fields of contraception, abortion, divorce, euthanasia, the gift of life—if the definition once given to them by the Church is considered to be intrinsically bound up with the Christian perception of existence. Hence the tendency to make certain ethical options more and more intransigent and absolute, on the grounds of the trouble that would be caused, for a certain number of Christians, by any kind of evolution in areas in which the official Church had made categorical pronouncements. The recent instruction issued by the Congregation for the Doctrines of the Faith on 'Respect for nascent human life and the dignity of procreation' is a characteristic example of this desire to tie up certain ethical stances with the Christian identity which is our heritage and which is not open to discussion. At the same time modifications are introduced into what is said to be inviolable. Thus, official pronouncements, moving imperceptibly from the notion of 'human being' to that of 'person', inculcate more and more the idea that a human person exists from the moment of conception, whereas one part of the Church's tradition, quite well supported, affirmed that human animation was not immediate.

3. In order to safeguard this Christian identity, not only at the level of a few great principles, but also in closely-defined patterns of behaviour, less and less attention is being paid in Christian ethics to meaning, intention, circumstances, personal experience—things which nevertheless represent a decisive dimension of every human action. Attention is concentrated on 'objective' standards, said to be ideal, which then become an absolute and complete point of reference for every concrete action.

By setting aside in this way the subjctive, more supple, more diverse aspects of complex ethical questions which cannot fully be grasped by *an exclusively 'objective' approach*, we end up with a somewhat materialistic moral judgment. Certain ethical stances of the official Church have, not without cause, sometimes been criticised on these grounds.

4. If Christian identity is established in relation to certain precise acts, defined in an abstract way, morality ceases to be a matter of ongoing dynamic decision-making on the part of individuals and communities—a dynamism that influences the way people live, inspired by the gospel message and the great human and Christian tradition. Morality becomes instead *an act of power*, a prerogative of authority.

No account is taken of what it means when people transgress or dispute (to dispute may be to bring to the attention of the community new values, or values that have not been sufficiently recognised). Both transgression and disputation are necessary if a society is to develop.

5. In order to guarantee and safeguard this Christian identity, it will be necessary to proclaim it by means of ethical judgments, categorically pronounced, 'in season and out of season'. It is this *proclamation*, rather than *experienced reality* which will prove most reassuring to the Christian public—pronouncements which aim to become more and more unanimous, even at the risk of being based on complete illusion.

Because the Church declares that marriage is indissoluble, many Christians are convinced that they are more faithful in marriage than non-Christians. This claim is far from being proved. It is reassuring when principles are forcefully enunciated, whatever may be their relation to reality. Maurice Blondel recently drew attention to our tendency to judge other people by their achievements, while we judge ourselves by our intentions.

The relevance of these principles which are enunciated will never be called into question, since what justifies them is not their impact on our way of life, but the fact that they are essential to our identity.

6. Such a codification of morality creates *the image of a God who is jealous of his sovereignty*, and who inscribes his precise intentions 'in nature', leaving hardly any place for human responsibility. This applies especially to the beginning and the final stage of existence. The route for our human journey has been laid down from the beginning of time in the mysterious purpose of God. Obedience to a *magisterium*, sole interpreter of the will of God, is moral virtue par excellence.

Such are some of the major obstacles and drawbacks which arise when Christian identity is located primarily in precise and detailed moral behaviour.

Yet Christians must be able to recognise themselves, to identify themselves, in the ongoing course of life. The coherence of a Church, as of any other community, needs concrete signs of belonging, of togetherness, of sharing in the same objectives, or commitment to the same options. Identity is necessary for the internal life of a Church, but it is equally indispensable if there is to be dialogue, confrontation or common action. It must be possible to recognise oneself, with one's own distinguishing marks and characteristics, if one is truly to operate at all the levels where individuals and groups with different tendencies are encountered.

2. MARKERS FOR AN ALTERNATIVE BASIS FOR CHRISTIAN ETHICS

1. Not every way of life can be reconciled with the gospel message. How could one follow Jesus without being concerned for the poor, without striving to bring more justice into all human relationships, without paying attention and respect to other people—to the stranger and the outcast, as well as to one's nearest neighbours? Some ways of living, then, are in harmony with the Christian faith, while others are incompatible with the Gospel.

But these moral options, essential for Christianity, are equally essential for others who do not share our view of the world. Because we have lived in a Christian universe, we have long thought that these values were peculiar to our faith. Even though it may be through my Christian education that I have discovered respect for other people, my sense of justice, or love for my neighbour, I am obliged today to recognise similar aspirations among non-Christians. This means that what is *essential* to us is not *necessarily exclusive* to us. And we have no right, as Christians, to claim a monopoly of those life-options which are part of the common heritage of humanity.

If there are entirely new perspectives in the behaviour and the teaching of Jesus, this does not mean that they are all peculiar to his message. Becoming part of history, Jesus takes over and adopts, in all their radicality, ways of life, cultural realities, and the values by which others also live. He thus identifies with that which is of the essence of human life, which is the exclusive property of none, but which is part of the common stock on which so many individuals and so many cultures try to draw. If we tried to appropriate it for ourselves, we would be depriving others of values, objectives, solidarities, which belong to them as much as to us.

Christians, who have grown accustomed to monopolising, in some measure, humanitarian values and institutions, need to try hard to restore them to humanity as a whole. Even if, in some cases, they have broken new ground, and done the work of pioneers, it is of vital importance that their membership of the Church should not set them apart from the great human family, whose quest and pilgrimage they share.

2. If we were to find it necessary to stop thinking ourselves better than others, to abandon the habit of claiming to be better than anybody else, in fact the sole experts in humanity, and were to stop trying (by our pronouncements rather than by our way of living) to teach the world lessons, where would we be? We would be travelling along with everybody else, feeling our way, and trying together to make this world of which we are a part more human. In doing this, we would be restoring its value to *God's first revelation in his creation*, which the coming of Jesus of Nazareth neither diminished nor rendered useless.

Jesus himself comes to the world as a fallow field, made available to all people of good will, so that they may make full use of all its possibilities. Would his closeness to the Father, and his messianic consciousness, have placed him automatically beyond the reach of all research, where he could not be tilled for the satisfaction of human needs? An important part of the teaching he left us is not linked with the religious dimension of our existence; it belongs rather to the fundamental humanity which is part of our common heritage, even if the concept of the Covenant with the God of Jesus Christ gives it extra force and breadth. We must not, therefore, as Christians, think that we are excused from the call, addressed to the depths of each person's heart, to work together with all people—in a combined effort of analysis and perceptiveness, of dialogue and solidarity—for the creation of a united humanity, at the heart of a reconciled universe.

Is our human condition, characterised as it is by a liberty which is in search of itself, which is maturing, which, little by little, is becoming more human, completely transformed by the coming of Jesus? Are there no longer any other ways for humanity than accepting his teaching, and belonging to the Church which his followers have set up? Is the quest for humanisation without reference to what is beyond humanity, totally without interest or value for the Christian, whose position now is quite different, and who no longer has anything to receive from the agnostic's or atheist's way of being human?

3. If, then, the absolute character of our moral choices is not confirmed by God's personal guarantee, what *firm basis and security can there be* for our actions?

Today there is no longer any moral judgment which is universally recognised as the only authorised expression of the ethical response required from individuals or from human societies. In a universe in which different perceptions of 'truth' and 'the good' clash with each other, the Christian community cannot ignore other ethical systems, and consider that it alone possesses moral truth. The conviction of the value of one's own choices should go hand in hand with a perception of complementary elements in the choices of others, making them sources of mutual enrichment. Henceforth it will be through *confrontation and ceaseless dialogue* between different conceptions of ethical values, and the obligations which flow from them, that humanity will be able to discover points of convergence, and so establish a wider basis for its moral values. Such confrontation will on the one hand make it possible for us to discern the limits of, and perhaps even the faults in, our own perceptions, and on the other hand bring confirmation of the merits of values recognised by different groups, starting from different premises.

Such permanent confrontation can only be real and effective if it is undertaken in serenity and humility, in confidence and mutual respect. We should feel sufficiently secure in our own perception to be able to call it into question and to enrich it with what comes from the convictions of others. This implies a dialogue between equals, where each one, freed from the conviction that he alone possesses the whole truth, can accept other approaches, and can himself be listened to as he presents his own scale of values, often based upon a long tradition.

It is the outcome of this ongoing confrontation, this common quest for more truth, and not the unrivalled authority of one or another, which will henceforth give confirmation and dynamism to ethical values.

3. A SPECIFICALLY CHRISTIAN CONTRIBUTION

Viewed in this way, does not Christian identity become so far attenuated that there no longer remains any kind of action that can be described as characteristic of the followers of Jesus?

In fact, since it is difficult to define the precise conduct required in the name of the gospel, and since doubt has been cast over the notion of a specifically Christian morality, a certain number of Christians are loyally committed to human struggles without any particular reference to their faith. Others, on the contrary, have a tendency to withdraw into a somewhat disembodied 'spiritual' realm, not concerning themselves with life's demands and problems, so as to avoid becoming involved in joint responsibilities which would certainly be sources of conflict. Should the ambiguity which is inherent in all involvement with others be seen, on the one hand, as an invitation to withdraw from the human struggle, or, on the other, as requiring the laying aside of one's religious convictions, so as to be able to engage in the struggle in loyal solidarity with all people of good will? On the contrary, the revealed message, culminating in the practice and the teaching of Christ, shows how completely the service of God and the service of our brothers are interwoven.

Witnesses to Transcendence

'Just as I have loved you, you also must love one another' (John 13:34). In speaking in this way to his disciples, is Jesus asking of them a love for their neighbour which is different from the love to which all are called? Are Christians required to do more than what is implied by care for others, respect, truth and justice in human relations? In other words, is there such a thing as a specifically Christian moral code, moral demands made on Christians alone, which would not be equally required of anyone concerned about humanity? Perhaps the phrase 'just as I have loved you' points to something other than different or better behaviour.

Is not that which is characteristic of the Christian to be found above all in the capacity to be fully involved in human reality, to be committed with everyone else and like everyone else to efforts to promote constantly the unity of the human race, while at the same time recognising a relationship with what transcends humanity?

The special contribution of the Christian is not to do something different, but to live out this human existence as a bearer of the reality of God, as the place where the God of Jesus Christ is present, as one who is animated by the breath of the Spirit. It is to take the risk of fully accepting the human condition, with all its calls for autonomy, freedom of enquiry, and responsible liberty, essential requirements for ethics, *while living a covenant relationship*. Why should God want to take anything away from human responsibility? Why should he want to supply ready-made answers to ethical questions which human beings have a duty to work out by drawing on their resources, helping one another, and learning the lessons of experience, happy or otherwise? By making his face shine on those who seek him, will God modify the demands, the responsibility and the greatness of the human condition, created so that it might build *itself* up?

Jesus of Nazareth, as bearer of the Jewish tradition, revealed to us in a new way and with a new sharpness the living God present in human history, infinite love magnetising human destiny, and so freeing it from fatalism and reviving its fundamental hope. This covenant dimension is acceptable only so long as it does not diminish in any way man's total acceptance of responsibility for his condition, his quest, his pilgrimage. A God who would want to deprive us of our full responsiblity is today no longer credible in the eyes of large numbers of people. In these circumstances, modern man, whether agnostic or even Christian, cannot accept, quite rightly, that a veto should be imposed on his research, for example into the beginnings of life, on the grounds that 'life belongs to God'. Such investigations must indeed have respect for human values, and must recognise the importance of prudence, clear-sightedness, and justice, but they cannot accept that human existence is subject to a divine sovereignty which would limit our responsible liberty.

When the modern world takes exception to the Christian, is it because of his faith in God, or his hope in a future life? Is it not rather when he tries, in the name of his religious faith, to impose on everybody his particular perspective of the human journey, when he dissociates himself from the common quest, when he either preaches submission to the established order, or else incites people to fanatical holy wars? Ought it not, then, to be possible to be fully integrated into the human condition, and to recognise in it a transcendent dimension which in no way severs the human being from his autonomy?

A pilgrim people

A second characteristic of the Christian is, or should be, his ability to return human achievements to the work-bench so that something better may be made of them. In this he is inspired by the life and teaching of Jesus, whose formative message is constantly challenging us, under the guidance of the Spirit, in new and disturbing ways. What Christ says—about not judging others, about accepting the marginalised, about money, about the relativity of the laws of the synagogue, about the place given to the destitute—is a call to us never to absolutise knowledge, the established order, or human hierarchies. Faced with the logic of God (for example in the story of the workers taken on by the employer at the eleventh hour, or in the Beatitudes, which are first and foremost, as J. Fr. Six has said, a revelation of God's way of doing things) we find that our prized human discoveries are constantly challenged and we are called, in a state of permanent *metanoia*, not to stop at closed certainties, of whatever kind they may be, but to continue on our way. This constant sending back to the work-bench does not render our researches and discoveries useless. Rather, it opens them up, and makes development possible.

Such permanent questioning is only possible if our human pilgrimage is sustained by hope: we are destined for completeness. The earthly paradise is not an initial gift; but it is present from the beginning of the journey, in the depths of human consciousness, as that which is to come, a possibility to work at, magnetising the history of each individual, and the history of humanity. Consequently everything must always be taken further. Not only our 'temporal' achievements, but also our religious practices, our institutional organizations, our doctrinal definitions. The Christian is a pilgrim.

To be fully involved in all one's human commitments, without ever absolutising any achievement, however valuable it may be, must be of the utmost importance for the way we understand 'Christian' ethics, or, more precisely, the contribution of Christians to human ethics.

It is right and good that Christians, the Christian community, should take their share in the moral effort of the world, both by their way of life, and by their declaration of values which seem to them to be of prime importance. In recognising that other people too can identify themselves with these values, Christians see important convergences between their own religious faith and the ways of life of others. Nevertheless, however useful the norms worked out by the Christian community may be, as markers for our journey, as a way of participating in the human community, as a translation into living experience of our belonging to the God of Jesus Christ, they can only have a relative, prudential character. They express ways of living inspired by the Christian conscience. But it is hard to see how, in their precise concrete forms, they can escape human conditionings of time and culture, and acquire, by a direct link with the gospel, an absolute character. If moral norms which, even if fashioned by the Church, remain a human development, became the ultimate standard of reference, what room would be left for the breath of the Spirit?

Discussions about the double nature in Jesus Christ will go on throughout Christian history without ever finding a fully satisfactory answer. It is impossible for us to understand how Jesus of Nazareth could at one and the same time share fully (apart from sin) in our human nature, and be divine. However, even if we do not fully grasp how they can be reconciled, we cannot abandon either of these dimensions of Christ. It is an essential part of our faith to believe that all that Jesus bore in himself of *divine belonging* in no way separated him from our human condition.

In his own measure, and in his own situation, the Christian faces a similar problem: how to perceive in what is human a transcendence which takes nothing away from the human condition. Here too, while we cannot grasp how these two components of human reality can be harmonised, we have to recognise this constantly creative presence of the eternal, while claiming not to lose in any way the values of responsible freedom, creativity, autonomy, and solidarity with everything human, which constitute our greatness and our particular identity.

That is the risk, that is the fundamental demand of ethics for the Christian.

Translated by G. W. S. Knowles

Christian Duquoc

Church Membership and Christian Identification

I VIVIDLY recall one of Magritte's paintings: A hermetically sealed window gives onto open countryside. A smashed pane is the only means of access. There was a hermetically sealed synod on the laity at Rome in October 1987. The journalists said nothing. A cardinal wrote that it was an 'indescribable experience'. From Magritte the painter to Gauchet the sociologist, who has just written a book called 'The Disenchantment of the World' (Paris 1986). The book has caused some excitement in France. The author up-ends the traditional theory of secularisation. He sees Christianity as fathering the western world. Christianity favoured technological science, inspired democracy, started the unceasing debate on pros and cons and why and wherefores, and supported the discontent which led to the renewal of attitudes and institutions. It is characteristic of Christian logic, given its profession of a God who as creator is absolutely transcendent, to effect a radical separation of world and God, and thus to commit mankind to responsibility. Paradoxically, belief in the incarnation of the Word reinforced the process which Judaism had already started. In the form of his substitute, God disputed the dreamed of messianic role and took the stance of a refusal of power—the Cross.

Hence God's withdrawal afforded human beings their own creative space. Quite unlike traditional religions which had anchored laws, rites and customs in an unchangeable origin, Christianity cancelled all links with the origin, and thus rejected all cosmic and divine systems which arrogated the right to decide the meaning of moral and political instances. Moreover, the immutability of traditional religions acted as a psychological prop, but Christianity by breaking with the origin and looking forward to an indeterminate future evoked anxiety. That unease is maintained inasmuch as Christianity, the metaphor of our very modernity, fulfils itself on the social plane, which means that it has to vanish as an external phenomenon, as, indeed, a Church. Henceforth Christianity takes our world as its substance. Of course inward faith may persist as the ultimate meaning of a mundane ethics and system of communication which necessarily remain transient. Modernity does not sound the death-knell of faith but individualises it and renders anachronistic an empirical Church which still claims to be the fount of social relations. Membership of the Church is no longer relevant in a secular world which fulfils the essence of Christianity while the Church continues to represent only an antiquarian form of that essence. 'Christian' identity is grounded either in the modern world or in social archaeology, and deserves the qualification 'Christian' only if it breaks with the institution.

Gauchet's thesis as outlined here is attractive. It offers a way into the dilemma referred to in the title of this article. To elucidate and perhaps solve it I shall divide my article into three parts: the problem itself; an evaluation of it; and future prospects.

1. THE PROBLEM

Gauchet's thesis may upset a believing Catholic. It is not so much his analysis of modernity which causes offence, for it is complimentary to Christianity. What is interesting is what may be called the sanctioning of success. Christianity is dying of its success. It is deprived of its social function and of its visible presence at the very moment when it is actually a social inspiration, and is suppressing its presence as Church. The individual can seek the Absolute but in the process does without church membership. The Church ceases to be a location of identity because of its now secular opposition to the process of modernisation. It lies as it were athwart the Christian path itself—across the dynamic process promised by Scripture which it nevertheless continues to proclaim. It reaches a state tantamount to schizophrenia, on the one hand by inspiring people to be creatively responsible in the world, and on the other hand by forcing people into archaic ethical and disciplinary moulds by rejecting any democratic discussion of matters which concern all baptized persons. The last synod is an example of this schizophrenia. On the one hand it supported without hesitation the struggle for equal men's and women's rights in civil society. Nothing can justify the exclusion of women from learning, political power, an equal voice in democratic debate, and equal pay. In this struggle for equality we may all see the effects of Christian logic. Christ has cancelled qualitative distinctions. On the other hand the Catholic Church rejects this equality in its visible organisation. The synod, in order to avoid any questioning of the place of women in the institution, spent much time on an anodyne text which said that it should be possible for little girls to sing in the choir—something already widely practised for the last ten years or more. In this way the officials of the institution take schizophrenia to an extreme. They demand for civil society rights and practices which they reject for the Church on the pretext that its secular discipline is immutable, for it is rooted in 'divine right'.

With what is the believer to identify? With the designs of a civil society which preaches—so the Church claims—an equality inspired by the gospel? Or with the institutional structure of the Catholic Church which justifies its anti-democratic organisation by appealing to 'divine right'? Which is the authentic source of identity? The dynamic process which is open to creative responsibility and to democratic discussion which is the essence of *Gaudium et Spes* (Vatican II), or the unchanging nature of the ecclesiastical organisation for which the Vatican bureaucracy is fighting? Is this a false dilemma? That remains to be shown. Is it a real one? Then believing Catholics must work to overcome it.

2. EVALUATION

There is a simple approach, and one which is often used, if we are to escape from the dilemma I have described in the foregoing. We may conceive empirical church membership as membership of the Church as the sacrament and Body of Christ. It is possible to maintain, of course, that membership of the Church as a means of Christian identification has nothing to do with the fantasies of the nostalgic individuals at ecclesial headquarters. The antiquarian or archaicising attitude of our officials is a minor trial of faith. One might add that the gap between ideal designs and actual management is a common experience of all societies and is to be found in political parties, trade unions and various associations which manifest similar contradictions. The Church exists elsewhere than in the narrow-minded thinking of its functionaries. We may leave them to play with theocracy. In all good faith they believe that they have God in their own hands, whereas they have nothing. God, in his Spirit, blows where he lists: he remains outside their calculations.

I think there is much virtue in this answer. It shows considerable detachment from unimportant issues. Yet it also treats lightly the suffering of numerous Catholics. They will not play down or underestimate the institutional presence of the Church and refuse to play any part in the archaic game. They think that certain forms of discipline run counter to the Gospel. In short, they think that an answer to this kind accords too neatly with Gauchet's thesis: henceforth Christianity is somewhere other than in the Church. Therefore they refuse to accept the practice of certain church officials in maintaining a distinction between the Church and the world which does not bear witness to the truth of the Kingdom of God.

This refusal to solve the dilemma by recourse to inwardness or to the realm of the invisible seems to me to be right, and shown to be right by recent ecclesiastical events. Some of those who rule us seem to have no ambition other than to render Vatican utterly banal. Their cause is the middle-of-the-road utterance or practice: discipline and symbolic forms which once were meaningful but are now oppressive, theologies which once were original but now fall flat. They are out to breathe life into what is dead, and are anxious to banish whatever is creative. Of course this strategy is conducted with holy zeal yet those responsible are always afraid, and their fear condemns them to pettiness.

If we accept that the Church, on the pretext that its true essence is not of this world, is to be governed by those who are prey to anxiety and fear, then we accept Gauchet's thesis: henceforth Christian identity is something apart from church membership because such membership deviates from the logic of Christianity. Only embittered individuals who cannot live without fixed reference-points will make the act of identification required by those who lead our Congregations. Free spirits will keep to the gospel. Schizophrenia no longer affects the individual, for he or she can choose his or her camp. It grasps the Church. I find this state of affairs difficult to accept. A few remarks on Gauchet's thesis and the present development of the Church will perhaps reveal another path.

The disappearance of the Church as the subject of a network of social relations and as a possible location for identification, as described by Gauchet, is certainly debatable on more than one ground. His thesis in fact depends on his definition of religion. According to him it represents the imperialism of the 'world apart'. Consequently, being logically destined to destroy this domination, if the Church wishes to remain loyal to that to which it bears witness, the Gospel, it has to work for its own destruction: it has to do all it can to cast off the very believers who are as it were welded to it.

Gauchet's thesis would be acceptable if the traditionalist bent was that of the vast majority. Catholic traditionalism, to be sure, was a major force from the period after the French Revolution, for many Catholics could find nothing compatible in the new mode of thought and the faith of their forebears. Though many leading churchmen may have held or at least entertained this viewpoint, it finally became clear that it was dangerous for the Church. What had been evident for some decades was openly declared by John XXIII when he summoned Vatican II. For this Pope it was a question of making the Church relevant to the modern world. Otherwise the message which it was the Church's mission to proclaim would not be heard. Vatican II awakened much hope even in circles which were relatively indifferent to religious questions. For many Catholics it was liberating. The council protected them from the schizophrenia which traditionalism sentenced them to. Identification through and with the Church was no longer contrary to what location in the modern world demanded. The anti-modern trend in the Catholic church had been leading to a sectarian and even fanatical mentality; it would have brought about the marginalisation of the Church. The about-turn achieved by Vatican II absolved attachment to the gospel and to the Church from all sectarianism. It emphasised a certain accord, in terms of the doctrine of the signs of the times, between the task of the Church and the thrust of the modern world. With Vatican II it was no longer necessary to state that one was anti-modern in order to identify oneself as a Christian. Now the Church no longer has to cancel its own presence in order to ensure that Christianity achieves its purpose. On the contrary, the logic of Christianity and that of the Church are of one and the same order. Therefore there is no longer any necessary connection between identity and a break with the world. Membership of the Church does not demand a secession from the world. New paths opened up with Vatican II.

But perhaps we are being far too optimistic if we see Vatican II as a reversal of the anti-modern strategy of the Catholic Church. Perhaps it would be a wrongheaded response to Gauchet's thesis on the disappearance of the Church in so far as it is archaic and antiquarian, to see Vatican II as a radical change of ecclesial practice. Does the post-Vatican II period show evidence of any verification of the hopes aroused more than twenty years ago? Was Vatican II anything more than mere wishful thinking? Has the post-Vatican II Church maintained the intention to emerge from sectarian seclusion?

Some recent options run the risk of pushing the Church once again into antiquarianism: the fascination of traditionalism for people who were much more liberated a while ago, the anxiety expressed by some representatives of the Roman Congregations, their dislike of change, their allergy to any creative initiatives in intellectual, pastoral and liturgical areas, their struggle against any episcopal tendency to autonomy, their manifest desire to repress anything which does not fit their ideas of orthodoxy, their icy enmity to dialogue and communication, and their devotion to immutability, risk consigning a *new* Church to the realm of folklore. Vatican II might prove to have been a fine parenthesis, a springtime, as in certain countries of the East, but with nothing to follow. Inertia and bureaucratic envy sanctioned by 'divine right' could suppress the burgeoning spirit. Could Gauchet be right in the end? Will Christianity cease to be relevant? The actions of some officials would seem to reveal such a conviction. But we are once again faced with the dilemma of identifying ourselves as Christian in spite of the Church or entering a sectarian universe. This is a dilemma I reject, for I can see other possibilities beginning to show through.

3. HOPE

In spite of its tendency to gloom, the last synod, as far as we can tell, did remember that the Church was the people of God. No one can challenge an idea which is the leading notion of the Vatican II constitution on the Church: 'Lumen Gentium'.

The stress on this idea seems to me to show an orientation to a Church which is neither sectarian nor antiquarian, a Church which can act as the location for identity without demanding that its members enter a schizophrenic state. There are four features which allow me to say that the Church may be a locus of positive identification: it is one way among others; it participates in democratic debate; it has a communitarian will; and it bears witness to a certain hope.

Before examining these four aspects, in order to avoid any misunderstanding, I must be more exact about what I mean by 'Church as community', though this demands a slight excursus from the course of my article. The notion of the Church as community is not all contrary to that of the Church as institution. It is a way of conceiving that institutional stance while remaining faithful to the definition of the Church as the people of God. The Church as institution is not something over against an invisible Church. They are both articulated in that the invisible Church is present as the openness and meaning of the Institution whose structure is defined by Word, Sacrament and government. But in my analysis, the Church as community is distinct from the bureaucratic manipulation of the Institution. Church bureaucratic instances concerned with helping and maintaining the work of bishops and their conferences develop their own kind of logic, even going so far as to diminish episcopal authority itself. The present way of appointing bishops, their doctrinal and disciplinary control by central instances, their lack of decision-making power in synods, and papal omnipresence in the media testify to the intention—supported by the ideological pressure of an unthinking devotion to the Holy See—to destroy the local episcopates' and their conferences' attempts to obtain a measure of respectful autonomy. The central bureaucratic control of the Institution is serious inasmuch as it conceives itself as serving the Church, when in fact it makes the Church its fief and disregards conciliar trends. The schematic or polemical character of some statements in the following pages arises from the situation of which the dilemma itself is evidence: who is responsible for church government—the bishops in union with the Bishop of Rome, or a centralising bureaucracy? In principle the constitution *Lumen gentium* resolved this dilemma.

(a) One way among others

Vatican II avoided the temptation to obtain Christian identity through sectarianism. We are not Christians by virtue of excluding or eliminating others. That is why the Council introduced reflection in the form of dialogue on ecumenism, Judaism and other religions. The meeting which John Paul II called at Assisi in October 1986 was a practical ratification of this tendency. The promises made to Israel and the Church are such that those who belong to such groups, because of their 'election', become members of an order of things which runs the risk of making them underestimate or despise those outside that order. In order to avoid this 'damnation' of those who are not members of the visible Church, Vatican II forcefully stressed the distinction between the empirical Church and the Kingdom of God. It was Augustine who affirmed the belief that 'many are outside who are actually inside, and many are inside who are actually outside'. The borderlines are not administrative. God did not restrict his grace and loving-kindness to the realm of the visible Church. This means at the very least that one does not enter the Church in the same way that one takes up membership of a political party, for one is never one with what the Church testifies to, which is the Reign of God. The visible Church, in its historical development, in spite of the sacraments and the word of Scripture, is full of ambiguities which affect any social entity and every individual. Christian identification is a process of conversion not to the Church but to the Kingdom. The Church itself must never cease to convert itself to what it is commissioned to bear witness to. Conversion does not mean conformity with a predetermined model, and the gospel does not provide such a model. It is a risk which we take in consciousness of present inadequacies. It does not exclude mistakes, ineptitudes and erros, but prevents commitment to them. The way of conversion is never complete and is the prime condition for an identity which neither patriotic, inflationist nor fanatical. It is a road of modesty and one which allows other roads to take their own course. The heart of God and of Christ is big enough for the Spirit to liberate the Christian from all pretension to superiority and scorn.

In fact, even in traditional theology, these are things which stand to reason. But group logic, when ecclesial, is an imperialist logic. The reasoning is simple:

if the Church is the locus of truth, others are in error and we have to liberate them from their error. Violence hovers nearby and has often entered in. It is more important to escape the complex of abstract problems associated with truth and universality: the Church is the witness to the way of Christ, and this way does not exclude other ways. God did not confer the right of judgment on the Church. He made it—in Christ—the location of powerlessness. He did not endow it as the sum of all knowledge. The conversion required of the Church amounts to a critique of natural group logic, to a refusal to be unique, in short to entering without reservations and without superiority into the democratic debate on the modes and problems of human life and survival.

(b) Engaging in democratic discussion

To exist as one way among others is the condition of ecclesial and individual conversion, and must be so if Christian identity is to avoid the danger of sectarianism or imperialism. This condition requires the Church to adopt a new, non-fanatical stance in debate: an opening of self towards the world and into it. The Church is not the only instance to examine human affairs and dilemmas, whether ethical or political, philosophical or religious. Entering a democratic discussion without any pretensions to being the ultimate instance (which necessarily leads to closure or domination) is the condition for a non-imaginary identification process.

The children of men do not acquire their personal identity—that is, their ability to communicate with others without self-destruction—by the sole act of self-consciousness. They achieve that status through the word of others, through the presence of third parties, and that presence, in the objectivity of language, defines and affirms society and culture. The child does not receive its specific identity from baptism alone. This is a potentiality signifying that without the word of an Other and the presence of a third party (the Church in this instance), it could not reach maturity. The group is therefore a locus of identification and is so by making communication possible. Anyone who remains closed makes a false act of self-identification. If the empirical Church rejects all discussion and appears only as the *magisterium*, how can it be a non-sectarian locus of identification? It is by entering into democratic discussion of these subjects which concern all men and women and without pretensions to the right to conclude the debate, that the Church can properly form the believer so that he or she becomes a witness to the Kingdom.

I was not amazed to read, at the end of the document entitled 'The Gift of Life', issued by the Congregation for the Teaching of Faith', that the task of the theologian and therefore of all believers who might bear witness, was to explicate the decisions of the *magisterium*, and at this juncture those of the

Roman Congregations. This definition corresponds analogically to the task of any intellectual in a totalitarian country. There the duty of an intellectual is to explain the Party's decisions. He or she has no other room for manoeuvre and no critical freedom. To enter the democratic discussion already implies a dereliction of his or her duty. The Party knows, whereas the intellectual disposes of this knowledge. The intellectual is the pliable tool of leading officials, for the decisions of these functionaries, in accordance with their situation in history, their class position, and divine guarantee, are always reasonable. They are spared any necessity for discussion. They do not have to encounter others. In the Church, this belief, which is rooted in zealous pursuit of the good, is the seed of violence. In other places and at other times, the relationship of zeal with power led to crime. The Inquisition was not an accident, but was grounded in the logic of absence of discussion. It was the result of the belief that the Church definitely shared in divine knowledge. But God, in his Son Jesus, was in the place of non-power: he was on the Cross. Thus the necessity of debate, because there is no non-pathological identity for human beings, if they hold ecclesial office which is not mediated by the word of others or a third-party instance. No one, not even the Church, has the right to take up the empty place which is the location of power and knowledge demanded by democratic discussion. The internal structure of the Church has to promote this modest requirement. Communitarian demands seem to postulate such a drive.

(c) A communitarian will

The Church cannot be one way among others or a partner in equal debate, if in its internal practice it does not bear witness to the requirements of openness and honesty which it proclaims to civil society and the political world.

The Church is not the Kingdom of God. It proclaims that Kingdom. It proclaims it not merely in a symbolical manner through Word and sacraments, but it anticipates it effectively, though very modestly, in the bonds woven between believers. It is primarily as community that it testifies to the imminence of the Kingdom. If the communitarian character of the Church is not visible and the Christian identification towards which it tends does not pass through the mills of open discussion, whatever rank one may enjoy; if festal happiness is grounded on a social existence which is essentially exclusive; and if different and even deviant people are not accepted, and are even excluded or despised, Christian identification will occur on the model of a totalitarian party. The ecclesial body will approximate to a predetermined model or practise exclusion. The bureaucracy which tends to affect all societies hates difference: it is something you cannot administer. The univocal is the deity of bureaucracy. But the one-track mentality does not sustain a community or a people, it organises a gang. The one-track mentality gives rise to banal argument because banality is its essence. A bureaucrat considers the essential only in the light of the banal. The bureaucratic system, in spite of Vatican II, continues to proliferate in the Catholic Church. It organises links between local churches and within local churches in the perspective of banality as the ultimate determining factor. Nothing is more destructive of community and therefore of communion than this confusion between the anodyne and the essential. It gives the Church a tedious and petty appearance.

Community exists only where there is debate and freedom. In this sense it is a process of conversion because the fulness of total being arises only through the sharing of solitary power. At present the Church remains a living tissue by virtue of the communities which are born in freedom and which act courageously. This phenomenon is less a matter of public awareness because our media of information speak almost exclusively about those who run the show. Hence we get something of a 'dual' Church: on the one hand living communities which are in the process of conversion to the gospel, and on the other hand a cold and niggling bureaucracy anxious to stay shut up in the realm of what has already been said and done. The Spirit has to work in this atmosphere of contradiction. The believer can choose his or her model for identification: cold obedience without any risk to the predetermined models of the administration, or a risky and continual process of conversion in a living whole for the sake of the Kingdom. Only the second of these two models, by very reason of its modesty, or its renunciation of power, is the locus of hope. It is the place where the ecclesial institution fulfils its raison d'être.

(d) A testimony of hope

Membership of the Church is a locus of Christian identification, but it is not so willy-nilly. Belonging to the Church is not some guarantee of a certificate of Christian identity. There is no 'ius solis' (a right which in many countries grounds one's nationality). Identification is a process which does not depend solely on the always possible failure of the believer, for it is also related to the historical status of the Church.

The Church has to endure a constant process of contradiction between its gospel perspective and its empirical burden. This contradiction is inevitable and is part of the historical status of the Church. The requirement of modesty arises from the reality of that status, for it is not an external moral imperative. The fact that the Church is one way among others, that it is required to act as an equal partner in democratic debate, and that it is a community which accepts differences and deviations, is part and parcel of its historical status. To wish to escape all that, would mean adopting an imaginary perspective and inducing believers to adopt a pathological identity. This modesty is related to the Church's status; it authenticates the appropriateness of its perspective, the Gospel, and the great stature of its hope.

Certainly one of the most intolerable sufferings which the believer must undergo is to discover through experience that the Church is not a locus of hope for inadequate believers, unbelievers and sometimes even militant believers. Instead it is seen as an obstacle, even for those who profess membership of it. Therefore the believer is seized by a contradiction. He or she makes a wager against the forces of death and against scepticism, and belongs to the Church because of that wager, because that is what the Church preaches: God in Christ has vanquished the forces of death on behalf of all of us. Yet the believer sees that the Church's organisational system is not experienced as a vital or liberating force but as an oppressive power, which can offer nothing for the future. The believer sees that increasingly the Church's cause is no longer experienced as the cause of God. The believer is a victim of this contradiction between the proclaimed Word, the affirmed hope and the effects of the system as they are experienced. If he or she is clear-headed then all will be the very test of faith. But if the believer asks questions about a univocal, uniform liturgy, marginalised creativity, the formal nature of the community, anonymity, the great principles which are continually proclaimed but never practised, the ruling tedium, the dominant banality, the mediocre moralism, and everything which goes to make up the countenance of the empirical Church for the onlooker and sometimes for the member, he or she must also ask whether all that is necessarily associated with the historical status of the Church. One of my fellow religious told me after the disappointment of the last synod that your faith had to be riveted to your body for you to stay in the system. The believer will deny that this mediocrity is part of the historical status of the Church, of the Institution, for he or she believes that in the thickets of this banality as it is experienced in so many places, there is evidence of gospel hope. The believer knows that bureaucracy is not part of the very being of the Church. Vatican II told him or her of the death of the system. Too frankly perhaps. He or she knows that the Spirit cannot be confined indefinitely in the administration of the anodyne and the banal, and that the Spirit does not labour at a mediocre hope, but is intent on opening up other spaces.

I am reminded once again of Magritte's picture with its broken pane. The bureaucratic system confines space, and tends to close people up in a law like the law of gravity, whose unrelenting nature Magritte represents by the figure of a soldier with his arms imprisoned in a brick wall. But hope prevails in all that, for the Spirit is above be and overcomes fate. The Spirit vanquishes the forces of death. The Church is not a clear-cut locus of identification. It is an ambiguous place, where the forces of death are at work in the guise of zeal and system, and the spirit labours in the shape of forces clothed in modesty and powerlessness. The Cross decides what leads to the Kingdom and what, disguised as solidity and permanence, is to be discarded as ephemeral. It is up to the believer, in the clarity of the Spirit and in loyalty to the Word, to decide which type of identity will form his or her way of belonging to the Church.

Translated by J. G. Cumming

PART V

Conclusion

Christian Duquoc

Conclusion: in the Interrogative

'A MAN never climbs higher than when he does not know where his path may lead him' says Nietzsche in his *Unseasonable Remarks*. The aim of this issue of *Concilium* is surely to refute such a proposition, you might say. It was indeed designed as a response to the stultifying indecision regarding Christian identity. Such indecision might be prompted by awareness of secular futility or of how the exalted pretensions of Christian belief have proved historically ineffective. Yet many believers think they are on a road whose destination they know well, one which marks them out as militant supporters or advocates of a certain cause, and one which sustains their conviction that they have a specific identity shared and acknowledged by other people.

After reading the contributions to this issue, Nietzsche's statement slips a doubt into my mind. Religious institutions, surely, are intent to impose a specific on a tentative identity. They know who I am, where I come from, and what my destiny is. A religious institution is the mirror in which I become conscious of a definite self. Without that mirror I would be on a road with an unknown destination. A religious institution tells me who I am. It declares that I am a member of a group with a clear purpose, and one whose word gives me an identity. I should only be led astray if I tried to be 'myself' apart from nomination by the group.

Thus we find calm, for the painful experience of identification seems to have been avoided. The religious institution manages finally to establish harmony between my subjective conviction of my own identity and my assured possession of objective truth. All I have to do is to abandon the impossible quest for my identity by handing myself over to the 'other'. Here, finally, I have been named and filed. My duties are defined; my hopes are gratified; everything is in order. Indecision is the product of wrong thinking. Preachers, ecclesiastical authorities, gurus, and the Pope himself know the right way. They labour to bind the evil spirit of wrong thinking. They work hard to maintain the fiction of knowing, a role which they act out explicitly in order to banish indecision and doubt about identity, and they imbue the institution or institutions which they control with that aim. For example, nothing is clearer to church authorities than the vocation and identity of a Catholic theologian. His duty is to demonstrate how necessary and reasonable the utterances of a responsible ecclesiastic are in his concern for the identity of the Christian people. If a theologian entertains doubts about the openness of the way whose destination is quite clear to authority, then his doubts are definitely the product of a bad spirit. They end in indecision. One finds one's identity in 'making common cause' with authority, even at the price of swallowing a fiction. Is that the authentic destiny of any ecclesiastical institution? When the 'others' outside the jurisdiction of such an institution register its and possibly their own disarray, does that legitimate its claim to know what identity really is?

'The wind blows where it wills, and you hear the sound of it, but you do not know whence it comes or whither it goes; so it is with everyone who is born of the Spirit' (John 3:8). This saying is designed to discourage the identity merchants. Nothing is more pleasurable for someone leading another along the paths of assured identity than choosing the Spirit's direction for him. An apparently simple device allows due authority to wriggle out of the discomfort which Jesus' words might otherwise cause it. The ruse is to define the aspect of Jesus' behaviour which is to be imitated, and to equate identity with Jesus with obedience to an authority or to a guru offering an unambiguous version of what Jesus commands. Following Jesus means following the Spirit; identifying with Jesus means having a Christian identity. Of course everything would be all right if only Jesus himself had not stressed the fact that his personal behaviour was not absolutely identical with the overall movement of the Spirit. The Spirit has not been commissioned to repeat *ad infinitum* what happened once. His task is to get rid of that kind of imitation so that each person can win through to his or her identity. Jesus would not have asked people to part from their father, from their mother, from their brothers and sisters, and from their wife, in order to put himself in their place by reinforcing the bonds of dependence. Imitating Jesus means attaining in the Spirit to a comparable freedom, to an analogous love to which no one can take some commonplace route, for it is unique.

Institutions dread this gospel originality. All the restorers of landscapes are convinced that they are working for the common good when they present the institutional Church as the clear locus of Christian identity. They hold that obedience to their decisions is the sole means of avoiding the indecisiveness of the scattered 'me' and of attaining to the unified 'I'. If the 'I' is the outcome of 'grief-work', the institutional guardians make it their business to sustain the process because they think they know the consequence. Their concern is understandable, but their very zeal casts suspicion on the Church. Are they working to aid the movement of the Spirit whose wantonness and spontaneity Jesus extolled? Concern for a proper identification surely leads to the military ideal as the model of the Church. A longing to cure indecision is recompensed with creative mediocrity. The present situation of 'roads which lead nowhere' offers Christians a chance to be what they are called to be: free spirits and not militants in a cause.

I can discern in those whose duty it is to watch over the birth of Christian freedom that unease which lurks behind their official actions: their paternal or maternal preoccupation makes them dread the consequences of an emancipation from their tutelary power.

No-one bestows identity; it is an unfinished task. The Spirit impels its challenge, while the institution would ward it off.

Translated by J. G. Cumming

Contributors

MASAO ABE is Russell Tolson Visiting Professor of Buddhist Studies at Pacific School of Religion, Berkeley, California, USA. A graduate of Kyoto University in Japan, he studied and practised Buddhism (especially Zen) with Sin'ichi Hisamatsu while also studying Western philosophy. As a Research Fellow of the Rockefeller Foundation he studied Christian Theology at Union Theological Seminary and Columbia University. He was Professor of Philosophy at Nara University of Education in Japan from 1952 to 1980. Since 1965 he has been visiting professor of Buddhism and Japanese philosophy in USA: at Columbia University, the University of Chicago, Princeton University, Claremont Graduate School, University of Hawaii, Haverford College and other universities.

Since the death of D. T. Suzuki Abe has been a leading exponent of Zen and Japanese Buddhism in the West. As a member of the Kyoto School of Philosophy, he is also deeply involved in the comparative study of Buddhism and Western thought and in Buddhist-Christian dialogue. His recent *Zen and Western Thought* (Macmillan and University of Hawaii Press) is a collection of essays on Zen in relation to Western thought. He also edited *A Zen Life: D. T. Suzuki Remembered* (Weatherhill). His many articles include: 'The Problem of Evil in Christianity and Buddhism in *Buddhist-Christian Dialogue* ed. Paul O. Ingram (University of Hawaii Press), 'The Problem of Time in Heidegger and Dogen' in *Being and Truth, Essays in Honour of John Macquarrie* ed. Alastair Kee (SCM Press), and 'Shinto and Buddhism: The Two Major Religions in Japan' in *The Scottish Journal of Religious Studies* Vol. VIII No. 1.

SCHALOM BEN-CHORIN was born in Munich in 1913, where he studied German and Comparative Religion. Moved to Jerusalem in 1935 where he now works as a writer, journalist and teacher, promoting progressive Judaism in Israel and Christian-Jewish dialogue. His principal works are: *Bruder Jesus*

(Munich 1967), *Paulus* (Munich 1970), *Mutter Mirjam* (Munich 1971), *Zwiesprache mit Martin Buber* (Munich 1966), *Germania Hebraica* (Gerlingen 1982), *Jüdischer Glaube* (Tübingen 1979), *Die Tafeln des Bundes* (Tübingen 1979), *Betendes Judentum* (Tübingen 1980), *Theologia Judaica* (Tübingen 1982), *Ich lebe in Jerusalem* (Gerlingen 1979), *Jugend an der Isar* (Gerlingen 1980), *Das weisse Licht* (Hamburg 1979).

PIERRE BÜHLER, Neuchâtel, Switzerland. Pierre Bühler was born in 1950 at Tramelan (Bernese Jura, Switzerland). He studied theology at Lausanne and Zurich. As assistant to Professor Gerhard Ebeling for several years, he obtained his doctorate under his supervision at Zurich in 1979 with a thesis on Luther's theology of the Cross. Since the autumn of 1982 he has been professor of systematic theology at the University of Neuchâtel where he is also director of the Institute of Hermeneutic and Systematic Research. Among his publications are: *Le problème du mal et la doctrine du péché*, Labor and Fides, Geneva; *Kreuz und Eschatologie. Eine Auseinandersetzung mit der politischen Theologie, im Anschluss an Luthers theologia crucis Mohr* (Tübingen 1981) doctoral thesis; *Justice en dialogue* Labor and Fides (Geneva 1982) collective work.

ISABELLE CHAREIRE was born in France in 1957. A lay woman, she studied philosophy at the State University of Lyon, submitting a Master's thesis on Hegel. After taking a further Master's degree in theology, she is reading for a third degree at the Catholic Faculties of Lyon, preparing a thesis on fundamental morality.

FRANÇOIS CHAVANNES was born at Lyons on 18 October 1922. He is a Dominican and has been assigned to the Algiers house since October 1953. Since 1965 he has had dual French-Algerian nationality. From August 1965 to November 1985 he was administrative assistant in the planning department of the Ministry of Agriculture in Algiers and took his theology degree at the Dominican le Saulchoir faculty in 1953. He has an IRFED diploma (Paris 1965). He has published various articles, especially on Camus' works. Since 1986 he has been working on a study of the questions which Camus' writings pose for Christianity.

CHRISTIAN DUQUOC OP was born at Nantes in 1926. He was ordained priest in 1953. He studied at the Leysse Dominican study centre in France, at Fribourg University, at the Dominican Saulchoir faculty in Paris, and at the Jerusalem Biblical School. He holds a diploma of the Biblical School and a doctorate in theology. He teaches fundamental theology in the Lyons theological faculty and is a member of the editorial board of *Lumière et Vie*. Among his publications are the two volumes of a *Christologie* (Paris 1972), *Jesus, homme libre* (Paris 1973), *Dieu différent* (Paris 1977), *Messianisme de Jésus et discretion de Dieu* (Geneva 1984), *Les églises provisoires* (Paris 1985), and *Libération et progressisme* (Paris 1987).

PETER EICHER, born 1943 in Winterthur, Switzerland, studied philosophy, literature, history and theology at Fribourg and Tübingen, gaining his D Phil in 1969 and D Theol in 1976. Since 1977 he has been professor of systematic theology (Catholic) at Paderborn. He is married with five children. Among his more recent publications are: *Das Evangelium des Friedens* (ed.) (Munich 1982); *Bürgerliche Religion. Eine theologische Kritik* (Munich 1983); *Theologie der Befreiung im Gespräch* (ed.) (Munich 1985); *Neues Handbuch theologischer Grundbegriffe* (ed.) four volumes (Munich 1984–85); *Karl Barth. Der reiche Jüngling* (ed.) (Munich 1986); (with M. Weinrich) *Der Gute Widespruch. Zum unbegriffenen Zeugnis von Karl Barth* (Düsseldorf/Neukirchen-Vluyn 1986).

PIERRE DE LOCHT was born in Brussels in 1916, and ordained priest in 1940. He received a doctorate in theology from the University of Louvain. From 1957 to 1958 he served as professor of theology in the theological faculty of Lovanium (Zaire). Since 1967 he has been a lecturer (now emeritus) in the University of Louvain. He is the author of a number of books and articles on ethical subjects.

ALPHONSE NGINDU MUSHETE was born in 1937 at Tshilundu in eastern Kasai. He studied at Kabwe minor seminary, and at the Mayidi major seminary (1960–65), then at the Lovanium, Louvain and Paris (Sorbonne) universities (1965–73). He took a degree in social sciences (1972). He was awarded his doctorate in theology in 1973 for a thesis on the problem of religious knowledge according to Laberthonnière. He is professor of dogmatic theology in the Catholic theological faculty at Kinshasa. He is one of the founders of the Ecumenical Association of Third-world Theologians (EATWOT) and since 1979 he has edited the *Bulletin of African Theology*, the official organ of the Ecumenical Association of African Theologians. His publications include articles on Laberthonnière, the unity and pluralism of theology, Christian faith and historical reason, African Christianity and the numinous in Africa.

THIERRY DE SAUSSURE was born in Geneva in 1934, and studied Protestant theology, psychology and religious psychology at the University of Geneva. He has been a psychoanalyst since 1971, is a member of the Swiss

Society of Psychoanalysts, and lectures at Geneva, Neuchâtel and Lausanne. He has published many articles, including studies of 'The Apostolic Formation of Priests', 'Guilt-feelings and the Meaning of Sin' and the application to Christian ethics of the relationship between psychoanalysis and Christianity.

CONCILIUM

1. (Vol. 1 No. 1) **Dogma**. Ed. Edward Schillebeeckx. 86pp.
2. (Vol. 2 No. 1) **Liturgy**. Ed. Johannes Wagner. 100pp.
3. (Vol. 3 No. 1) **Pastoral**. Ed. Karl Rahner. 104pp.
4. (Vol. 4 No. 1) **Ecumenism**. Hans Küng. 108pp.
5. (Vol. 5 No. 1) **Moral Theology**. Ed. Franz Bockle. 98pp.
6. (Vol. 6 No. 1) **Church and World**. Ed. Johannes Baptist Metz. 92pp.
7. (Vol. 7 No. 1) **Church History**. Roger Aubert. 92pp.
8. (Vol. 8 No. 1) **Canon Law**. Ed. Teodoro Jimenez Urresti and Neophytos Edelby. 96pp.
9. (Vol. 9 No. 1) **Spirituality**. Ed. Christian Duquoc. 88pp.
10. (Vol. 10 No. 1) **Scripture**. Ed. Pierre Benoit and Roland Murphy. 92pp.
11. (Vol. 1 No. 2) **Dogma**. Ed. Edward Shillebeeckx. 88pp.
12. (Vol. 2 No. 2) **Liturgy**. Ed. Johannes Wagner. 88pp.
13. (Vol. 3 No. 2) **Pastoral**. Ed. Karl Rahner. 84pp.
14. (Vol. 4 No. 2) **Ecumenism**. Ed. Hans Küng. 96pp.
15. (Vol. 5 No. 2) **Moral Theology**. Ed. Franz Bockle. 88pp.
16. (Vol. 6 No. 2) **Church and World**. Ed. Johannes Baptist Metz. 84pp.
17. (Vol. 7 No. 2) **Church History**. Ed. Roger Aubert. 96pp.
18. (Vol. 8 No. 2) **Religious Freedom**. Ed. Neophytos Edelby and Teodoro Jimenez Urresti. 96pp.
19. (Vol. 9 No. 2) **Religionless Christianity?** Ed. Christian Duquoc. 96pp.
20. (Vol. 10 No. 2) **The Bible and Tradition**. Ed. Pierre Benoit and Roland E. Murphy. 96pp.
21. (Vol. 1 No. 3) **Revelation and Dogma**. Ed. Edward Schillebeeckx. 88pp.
22. (Vol. 2 No. 3) **Adult Baptism and Initiation**. Ed. Johannes Wagner. 96pp.
23. (Vol. 3 No. 3) **Atheism and Indifference**. Ed. Karl Rahner. 92pp.
24. (Vol. 4 No. 3) **The Debate on the Sacraments**. Ed. Hans Küng. 92pp.
25. (Vol. 5 No. 3) **Morality, Progress and History**. Ed. Franz Bockle. 84pp.
26. (Vol. 6 No. 3) **Evolution**. Ed. Johannes Baptist Metz. 88pp.
27. (Vol. 7 No. 3) **Church History**. Ed. Roger Aubert. 92pp.
28. (Vol. 8 No. 3) **Canon Law—Theology and Renewal**. Ed. Neophytos Edelby and Teodoro Jimenez Urresti. 92pp.
29. (Vol. 9 No. 3) **Spirituality and Politics**. Ed. Christian Duquoc. 84pp.
30. (Vol. 10 No. 3) **The Value of the Old Testament**. Ed. Pierre Benoit and Roland Murphy. 92pp.
31. (Vol. 1 No. 4) **Man, World and Sacrament**. Ed. Edward Schillebeeckx. 84pp.
32. (Vol. 2 No. 4) **Death and Burial: Theology and Liturgy**. Ed. Johannes Wagner. 88pp.
33. (Vol. 3 No. 4) **Preaching the Word of God**. Ed. Karl Rahner. 96pp.
34. (Vol. 4 No. 4) **Apostolic by Succession?** Ed. Hans Küng. 96pp.
35. (Vol. 5 No. 4) **The Church and Social Morality**. Ed. Franz Bockle. 92pp.
36. (Vol. 6 No. 4) **Faith and the World of Politics**. Ed. Johannes Baptist Metz. 96pp.
37. (Vol. 7 No. 4) **Prophecy**. Ed. Roger Aubert. 80pp.
38. (Vol. 8 No. 4) **Order and the Sacraments**. Ed. Neophytos Edelby and Teodoro Jimenez Urresti. 96pp.
39. (Vol. 9 No. 4) **Christian Life and Eschatology**. Ed. Christian Duquoc. 94pp.
40. (Vol. 10 No. 4) **The Eucharist: Celebrating the Presence of the Lord**. Ed. Pierre Benoit and Roland Murphy. 88pp.
41. (Vol. 1 No. 5) **Dogma**. Ed. Edward Schillebeeckx. 84pp.
42. (Vol. 2 No. 5) **The Future of the Liturgy**. Ed. Johannes Wagner. 92pp.
43. (Vol. 3 No. 5) **The Ministry and Life of Priests Today**. Ed. Karl Rahner. 104pp.
44. (Vol. 4 No. 5) **Courage Needed**. Ed. Hans Küng. 92pp.
45. (Vol. 5 No. 5) **Profession and Responsibility in Society**. Ed. Franz Bockle. 84pp.
46. (Vol. 6 No. 5) **Fundamental Theology**. Ed. Johannes Baptist Metz. 84pp.
47. (Vol. 7 No. 5) **Sacralization in the History of the Church**. Ed. Roger Aubert. 80pp.
48. (Vol. 8 No. 5) **The Dynamism of Canon Law**. Ed. Neophytos Edelby and Teodoro Jimenez Urresti. 92pp.
49. (Vol. 9 No. 5) **An Anxious Society Looks to the Gospel**. Ed. Christian Duquoc. 80pp.
50. (Vol. 10 No. 5) **The Presence and Absence of God**. Ed. Pierre Benoit and Roland Murphy. 88pp.
51. (Vol. 1 No. 6) **Tension between Church and Faith**. Ed. Edward Schillebeeckx. 160pp.
52. (Vol. 2 No. 6) **Prayer and Community**. Ed. Herman Schmidt. 156pp.
53. (Vol. 3 No. 6) **Catechetics for the Future**. Ed. Alois Müller. 168pp.
54. (Vol. 4 No. 6) **Post-Ecumenical Christianity**. Ed. Hans Küng. 168pp.
55. (Vol. 5 No. 6) **The Future of Marriage as Institution**. Ed. Franz Bockle. 180pp.
56. (Vol. 6 No. 6) **Moral Evil Under Challenge**. Ed. Johannes Baptist Metz. 160pp.
57. (Vol. 7 No. 6) **Church History at a Turning Point**. Ed. Roger Aubert. 160pp.
58. (Vol. 8 No. 6) **Structures of the Church's Presence in the World of Today**. Ed. Teodoro Jimenez Urresti. 160pp.
59. (Vol. 9 No. 6) **Hope**. Ed. Christian Duquoc. 160pp.
60. (Vol. 10 No. 6) **Immortality and Resurrection**. Ed. Pierre Benoit and Roland Murphy. 160pp.
61. (Vol. 1 No. 7) **The Sacramental Administration of Reconciliation**. Ed. Edward Schillebeeckx. 160pp.
62. (Vol. 2 No. 7) **Worship of Christian Man Today**. Ed. Herman Schmidt. 156pp.
63. (Vol. 3 No. 7) **Democratization of the Church**. Ed. Alois Müller. 160pp.
64. (Vol. 4 No. 7) **The Petrine Ministry in the Church**. Ed. Hans Küng. 160pp.
65. (Vol. 5 No. 7) **The Manipulation of Man**. Ed. Franz Bockle. 144pp.
66. (Vol. 6 No. 7) **Fundamental Theology in the Church**. Ed. Johannes Baptist Metz. 156pp.
67. (Vol. 7 No. 7) **The Self-Understanding of the Church**. Ed. Roger Aubert. 144pp.
68. (Vol. 8 No. 7) **Contestation in the Church**. Ed. Teodoro Jimenez Urresti. 152pp.
69. (Vol. 9 No. 7) **Spirituality, Public or Private?** Ed. Christian Duquoc. 156pp.
70. (Vol. 10 No. 7) **Theology, Exegesis and Proclamation**. Ed. Roland Murphy. 144pp.
71. (Vol. 1 No. 8) **The Bishop and the Unity of the Church**. Ed. Edward Schillebeeckx. 156pp.
72. (Vol. 2 No. 8) **Liturgy and the Ministry**. Ed. Herman Schmidt. 160pp.
73. (Vol. 3 No. 8) **Reform of the Church**. Ed. Alois Müller and Norbert Greinacher. 152pp.
74. (Vol. 4 No. 8) **Mutual Recognition of Ecclesial Ministries?** Ed. Hans Küng and Walter Kasper. 152pp.
75. (Vol. 5 No. 8) **Man in a New Society**. Ed. Franz Bockle. 160pp.
76. (Vol. 6 No. 8) **The God Question**. Ed. Johannes Baptist Metz. 156pp.
77. (Vol. 7 No. 8) **Election-Consensus-Reception**. Ed. Giuseppe Alberigo and Anton Weiler. 156pp.
78. (Vol. 8 No. 8) **Celibacy of the Catholic Priest**. Ed. William Bassett and Peter Huizing. 160pp.
79. (Vol. 9 No. 8) **Prayer**. Ed. Christian Duquoc and Claude Geffré. 126pp.
80. (Vol. 10 No. 8) **Ministries in the Church**. Ed. Bas van Iersel and Roland Murphy. 152pp.
81. **The Persistence of Religion**. Ed. Andrew Greeley and Gregory Baum. 0 8164 2537 X 168pp.
82. **Liturgical Experience of Faith**. Ed. Herman Schmidt and David Power. 0 8164 2538 8 144pp.
83. **Truth and Certainty**. Ed. Edward Schillebeeckx and Bas van Iersel. 0 8164 2539 6 144pp.
84. **Political Commitment and Christian Community**. Ed. Alois Müller and Norbert Greinacher. 0 8164 2540 X 156pp.
85. **The Crisis of Religious Language**. Ed. Johannes Baptist Metz and Jean-Pierre Jossua. 0 8164 2541 8 144pp.
86. **Humanism and Christianity**. Ed. Claude Geffré. 0 8164 2542 6 144pp.
87. **The Future of Christian Marriage**. Ed. William Bassett and Peter Huizing. 0 8164 2575 2.

88. **Polarization in the Church.** Ed. Hans Küng and Walter Kasper. 0 8164 2572 8 156pp.
89. **Spiritual Revivals.** Ed. Christian Duquoc and Casiano Floristán. 0 8164 2573 6 156pp.
90. **Power and the Word of God.** Ed. Franz Bockle and Jacques Marie Pohier. 0 8164 2574 4 156pp.
91. **The Church as Institution.** Ed. Gregory Baum and Andrew Greeley. 0 8164 2575 2 168pp.
92. **Politics and Liturgy.** Ed. Herman Schmidt and David Power. 0 8164 2576 0 156pp.
93. **Jesus Christ and Human Freedom.** Ed. Edward Schillebeeckx and Bas van Iersel. 0 8164 2577 9 168pp.
94. **The Experience of Dying.** Ed. Norbert Greinacher and Alois Müller. 0 8164 2578 7 156pp.
95. **Theology of Joy.** Ed. Johannes Baptist Metz and Jean-Pierre Jossua. 0 8164 2579 5 164pp.
96. **The Mystical and Political Dimension of the Christian Faith.** Ed. Claude Geffré and Gustavo Guttierez. 0 8164 2580 9 168pp.
97. **The Future of the Religious Life.** Ed. Peter Huizing and William Bassett. 0 8164 2094 7 96pp.
98. **Christians and Jews.** Ed. Hans Küng and Walter Kasper. 0 8164 2095 5 96pp.
99. **Experience of the Spirit.** Ed. Peter Huizing and William Bassett. 0 8164 2096 3 144pp.
100. **Sexuality in Contemporary Catholicism.** Ed. Franz Bockle and Jacques Marie Pohier. 0 8164 2097 1 126pp.
101. **Ethnicity.** Ed. Andrew Greeley and Gregory Baum. 0 8164 2145 5 120pp.
102. **Liturgy and Cultural Religious Traditions.** Ed. Herman Schmidt and David Power. 0 8164 2146 2 120pp.
103. **A Personal God?** Ed. Edward Schillebeeckx and Bas van Iersel. 0 8164 2149 8 142pp.
104. **The Poor and the Church.** Ed. Norbert Greinacher and Alois Müller. 0 8164 2147 1 128pp.
105. **Christianity and Socialism.** Ed. Johannes Baptist Metz and Jean-Pierre Jossua. 0 8164 2148 X 144pp.
106. **The Churches of Africa: Future Prospects.** Ed. Claude Geffré and Bertrand Luneau. 0 8164 2150 1 128pp.
107. **Judgement in the Church.** Ed. William Bassett and Peter Huizing. 0 8164 2166 8 128pp.
108. **Why Did God Make Me?** Ed. Hans Küng and Jürgen Moltmann. 0 8164 2167 6 112pp.
109. **Charisms in the Church.** Ed. Christian Duquoc and Casiano Floristán. 0 8164 2168 4 128pp.
110. **Moral Formation and Christianity.** Ed. Franz Bockle and Jacques Marie Pohier. 0 8164 2169 2 120pp.
111. **Communication in the Church.** Ed. Gregory Baum and Andrew Greeley. 0 8164 2170 6 126pp.
112. **Liturgy and Human Passage.** Ed. David Power and Luis Maldonado. 0 8164 2608 2 136pp.
113. **Revelation and Experience.** Ed. Edward Schillebeeckx and Bas van Iersel. 0 8164 2609 0 134pp.
114. **Evangelization in the World Today.** Ed. Norbert Greinacher and Alois Müller. 0 8164 2610 4 136pp.
115. **Doing Theology in New Places.** Ed. Jean-Pierre Jossua and Johannes Baptist Metz. 0 8164 2611 2 120pp.
116. **Buddhism and Christianity.** Ed. Claude Geffré and Mariasusai Dhavamony. 0 8164 2612 0 136pp.
117. **The Finances of the Church.** Ed. William Bassett and Peter Huizing. 0 8164 2197 8 160pp.
118. **An Ecumenical Confession of Faith?** Ed. Hans Küng and Jürgen Moltmann. 0 8164 2198 6 136pp.
119. **Discernment of the Spirit and of Spirits.** Ed. Casiano Floristán and Christian Duquoc. 0 8164 2199 4 136pp.
120. **The Death Penalty and Torture.** Ed. Franz Bockle and Jacques Marie Pohier. 0 8164 2200 1 136pp.
121. **The Family in Crisis or in Transition.** Ed. Andrew Greeley. 0 567 30001 3 128pp.
122. **Structures of Initiation in Crisis.** Ed. Luis Maldonado and David Power. 0 567 30002 1 128pp.
123. **Heaven.** Ed. Bas van Iersel and Edward Schillebeeckx. 0 567 30003 X 120pp.
124. **The Church and the Rights of Man.** Ed. Alois Müller and Norbert Greinacher. 0 567 30004 8 140pp.
125. **Christianity and the Bourgeoisie.** Ed. Johannes Baptist Metz. 0 567 30005 6 144pp.
126. **China as a Challenge to the Church.** Ed. Claude Geffré and Joseph Spae. 0 567 30006 4 136pp.
127. **The Roman Curia and the Communion of Churches.** Ed. Peter Huizing and Knut Walf. 0 567 30007 2 144pp.
128. **Conflicts about the Holy Spirit.** Ed. Hans Küng and Jürgen Moltmann. 0 567 30008 0 144pp.
129. **Models of Holiness.** Ed. Christian Duquoc and Casiano Floristán. 0 567 30009 9 128pp.
130. **The Dignity of the Despised of the Earth.** Ed. Jacques Marie Pohier and Dietmar Mieth. 0 567 30010 2 144pp.
131. **Work and Religion.** Ed. Gregory Baum. 0 567 30011 0 148pp.
132. **Symbol and Art in Worship.** Ed. Luis Maldonado and David Power. 0 567 30012 9 136pp.
133. **Right of the Community to a Priest.** Ed. Edward Schillebeeckx and Johannes Baptist Metz. 0 567 30013 7 148pp.
134. **Women in a Men's Church.** Ed. Virgil Elizondo and Norbert Greinacher. 0 567 30014 5 144pp.
135. **True and False Universality of Christianity.** Ed. Claude Geffré and Jean-Pierre Jossua. 0 567 30015 3 138pp.
136. **What is Religion? An Inquiry for Christian Theology.** Ed. Mircea Eliade and David Tracy. 0 567 30016 1 98pp.
137. **Electing our Own Bishops.** Ed. Peter Huizing and Knut Walf. 0 567 30017 X 112pp.
138. **Conflicting Ways of Interpreting the Bible.** Ed. Hans Küng and Jürgen Moltmann. 0 567 30018 8 112pp.
139. **Christian Obedience.** Ed. Casiano Floristán and Christian Duquoc. 0 567 30019 6 96pp.
140. **Christian Ethics and Economics: the North-South Conflict.** Ed. Dietmar Mieth and Jacques Marie Pohier. 0 567 30020 X 128pp.
141. **Neo-Conservatism: Social and Religious Phenomenon.** Ed. Gregory Baum and John Coleman. 0 567 30021 8.
142. **The Times of Celebration.** Ed. David Power and Mary Collins. 0 567 30022 6.
143. **God as Father.** Ed. Edward Schillebeeckx and Johannes Baptist Metz. 0 567 30023 4.
144. **Tensions Between the Churches of the First World and the Third World.** Ed. Virgil Elizondo and Norbert Greinacher. 0 567 30024 2.
145. **Nietzsche and Christianity.** Ed. Claude Geffré and Jean-Pierre Jossua. 0 567 30025 0.
146. **Where Does the Church Stand?** Ed. Giuseppe Alberigo. 0 567 30026 9.
147. **The Revised Code of Canon Law: a Missed Opportunity?** Ed. Peter Huizing and Knut Walf. 0 567 30027 7.
148. **Who Has the Say in the Church?** Ed. Hans Küng and Jürgen Moltmann. 0 567 30028 5.
149. **Francis of Assisi Today.** Ed. Casiano Floristán and Christian Duquoc. 0 567 30029 3.
150. **Christian Ethics: Uniformity, Universality, Pluralism.** Ed. Jacques Pohier and Dietmar Mieth. 0 567 30030 7.
151. **The Church and Racism.** Ed. Gregory Baum and John Coleman. 0 567 30031 5.
152. **Can we always celebrate the Eucharist?** Ed. Mary Collins and David Power. 0 567 30032 3.
153. **Jesus, Son of God?** Ed. Edward Schillebeeckx and Johannes-Baptist Metz. 0 567 30033 1.
154. **Religion and Churches in Eastern Europe.** Ed. Virgil ELizondo and Norbert Greinacher. 0 567 30034 X.
155. **'The Human', Criterion of Christian Existence?** Ed. Claude Geffré and Jean-Pierre Jossua. 0 567 30035 8.
156. **The Challenge of Psychology to Faith.** Ed. Steven Kepnes (Guest Editor) and David Tracy. 0 567 30036 6.
157. **May Church Ministers be Politicians?** Ed. Peter Huizing and Knut Walf. 0 567 30037 4.
158. **The Right to Dissent.** Ed. Hans Küng and Jürgen Moltmann. 0 567 30038 2.

CONCILIUM

159. **Learning to pray.** Ed. Casiano Floristán and Christian Duquoc. 0 567 30039 0.
160. **Unemployment and the Right to Work.** Ed. Dietmar Mieth and Jacques Pohier. 0 567 30040 4.
161. **New Religious Movements.** Ed. by John Coleman and Gregory Baum.
162. **Liturgy: A Creative Tradition.** Ed. by Mary Collins and David Power.
163. **Martyrdom Today.** Ed. by Johannes-Baptist Metz and Edward Schillebeeckx.
164. **Church and Peace.** Ed. by Virgil Elizondo and Norbert Greinacher.
165. **Indifference to Religion.** Ed. by Claude Geffré and Jean-Pierre Jossua.
166. **Theology and Cosmology.** Ed. by David Tracy and Nicholas Lash.
167. **The Ecumenical Council and the Church Constitution.** Ed. by Peter Huizing and Knut Walf.
168. **Mary in the Churches.** Ed. by Hans Küng and Jürgen Moltmann.
169. **Job and the Silence of God.** Ed. by Christian Duquoc and Casiano Floristán.
170. **Twenty Years of Concilium—Retrospect and Prospect.** Ed. by Edward Schillebeeckx, Paul Brand and Anton Weiler.
171. **Different Theologies, Common Responsibility: Babel or Pentecost?** Ed. by C. Geffré, G. Gutierrez, V. Elizondo.
172. **The Ethics of Liberation—The Liberation of Ethics.** Ed. by D. Mieth, J. Pohier.
173. **The Sexual Revolution.** Ed. by Baum, J. Coleman.
174. **The Transmission of the Faith to the Next Generation.** Ed. by V. Elizondo, D. Tracy.
175. **The Holocaust as Interruption.** Ed. by E. Fiorenza, D. Tracy.
176. **La Iglesia Popular: Between Fear and Hope.** Ed. by L. Boff, V. Elizondo.
177. **Monotheism.** Ed. by Claude Geffré and Jean Pierre Jossua.
178. **Blessing and Power.** Ed. by David Power and Mary Collins.
179. **Suicide and the Right to Die.** Ed. by Jacques Pohier and Dietmar Mieth.
180. **The Teaching Authority of the Believers.** Ed. by Johannes-Baptist Metz and Edward Schillebeeckx.
181. **Youth Without a Future?** Ed. by John Coleman and Gregory Baum.
182. **Women—Invisible in Church and Theology.** Ed. by Elisabeth Fiorenza and Mary Collins.
183. **Christianity Among World Religions.** Ed. by Hans Küng and Jürgen Moltmann.
184. **Forgiveness.** Ed. by Casiano Floristán and Christian Duquoc.
185. **Canon Law—Church Reality.** Ed. by James Provost and Knut Walf.
186. **Popular Religion.** Ed. by Norbert Greinacher and Norbert Mette.
187. **Option for the Poor! Challenge to the Rich Countries.** Ed. by Leonardo Boff and Virgil Elizondo.
188. **Synod 1985: An Evaluation.** Ed. by Giuseppe Alberigo and James Provost.

CONCILIUM 1987

THE EXODUS
Edited by Bas van Iersel and Anton Weiler — 189

THE FATE OF CONFESSION
Edited by Mary Collins and David Power — 190

CHANGING VALUES AND VIRTUES
Edited by Dietmar Mieth and Jacques Pohier — 191

ORTHODOXY AND HETERODOXY
Edited by Johannes-Baptist Metz and Edward Schillebeeckx — 192

THE CHURCH AND CHRISTIAN DEMOCRACY
Edited by Gregory Baum and John Coleman — 193

WOMEN, WORK AND POVERTY
Edited by Elisabeth Schüssler Fiorenza and Anne Carr — 194

All back issues are still in print: available from bookshops (price £5.45) or direct from the publishers (£5.95/US$9.95/Can$11.75 including postage and packing).

T & T CLARK LTD, 59 GEORGE STREET, EDINBURGH EH2 2LQ, SCOTLAND

SUBSCRIBE TO CONCILIUM

'**CONCILIUM** a journal of world standing, is far and away the best.'
The Times

'... it is certainly the most variegated and stimulating school of theology active today. **CONCILIUM** ought to be available to all clergy and layfolk who are anxious to keep abreast of what is going on in the theological workshops of the world today.'
Theology

CONCILIUM is published on the first of every alternate month beginning in February. Over twelve issues (two years), themes are drawn from the following key areas: dogma, liturgy, pastoral theology, ecumenism, moral theology, the sociology of religion, Church history, canon law, spirituality, scripture, Third World theology and Feminist theology (see back cover for details of 1988 titles). As a single issue sells for £5.45 a subscription can mean savings of up to £12.75.

SUBSCRIPTION RATES 1988

	UK	USA	Canada	Other Countries
New Subscribers	£19.95	$39.95	$49.95	£19.95
Regular Subscribers	£27.50	$49.95	$59.95	£27.50
Airmail		$65.00	$79.95	£37.50

All prices include postage and packing. **CONCILIUM** is sent 'accelerated surface post' to the USA and Canada and by surface mail to other destinations.

Cheques payable to T & T Clark. Personal cheques in $ currency acceptable. Credit card payments by *Access*, *Mastercard* and *Visa*.

'A bold and confident venture in contemporary theology. All the best new theologians are contributing to this collective summa'.
Commonweal

Send your order direct to the Publishers

T & T CLARK LTD   59 GEORGE STREET
                           EDINBURGH
                           EH2 2LQ
Publishers   since 1821   SCOTLAND